• Die Sprachzeitung •

Trainingsheft

Charts & Co.

Describing and Analysing Visuals

by Rebecca Kaplan

Carl Ed. Schünemann KG

Table of Contents

BAR CHARTS

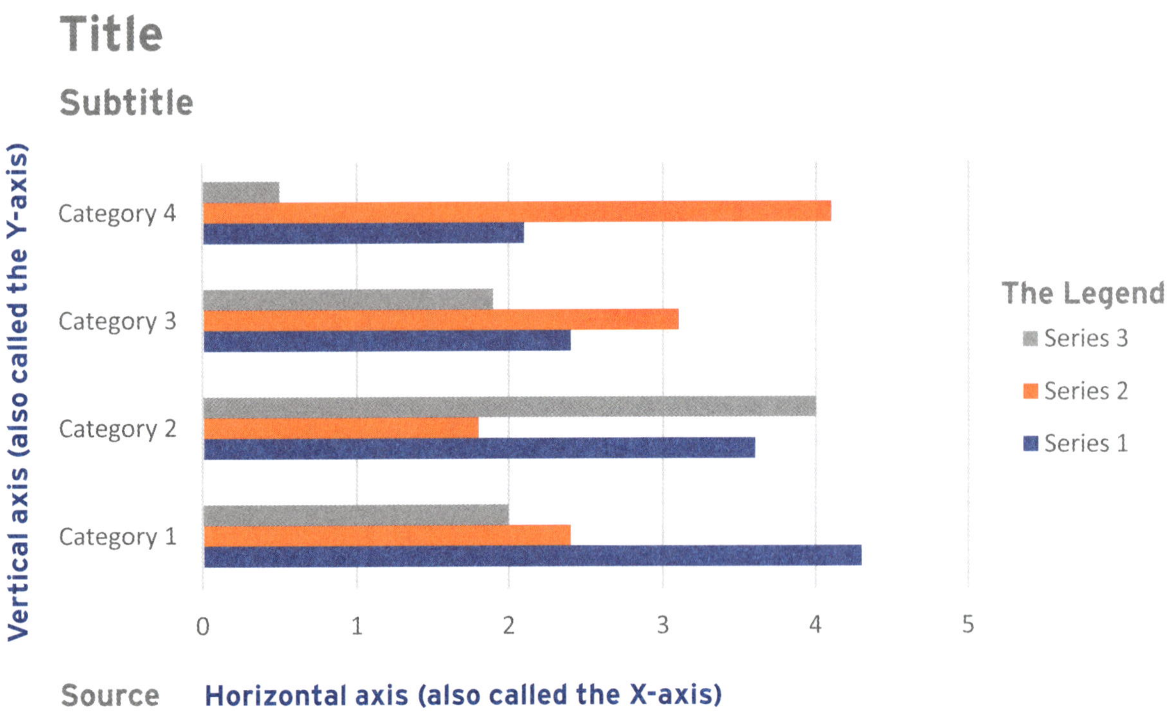

FACT FILE

A bar chart compares the size or number of different categories, items, or things. There may be more than one item in each category. The bars can be either vertical or horizontal. Vertical bar charts are sometimes called column charts.

— One axis shows the categories being compared. The other shows size, amount, or other values.

— Some bar charts, like the one above, show groups of bars. These are called 'multiple bar charts'.

— The heights and lengths of the bars are proportional to their values. A longer or higher bar means a larger or smaller value. You can quickly see which things in the chart are larger or smaller.

bar Balken — **chart; graph** Diagramm — **column** Säule — **axis** Achse — **value** Wert — **multiple** mehrfach — **unit** Einheit

GUIDELINES FOR DESCRIBING AND ANALYSING A BAR CHART

— What type of bar chart is it?
It's a simple / multiple bar chart / column chart / …

— What is on each axis? What are the units (time, number or amount of people or things, money, etc.)?
The vertical axis (Y-axis) shows the number (%) / amount of / size …
The horizontal axis (X-axis) shows the categories …

— What does each bar show? What's the colour of each bar (if there is more than one colour)?
Each bar shows …
The yellow bar is for … It shows …

BAR CHART 1

Guided

America's Favourite* Fourth of July Foods

US / Culture / Food / Business

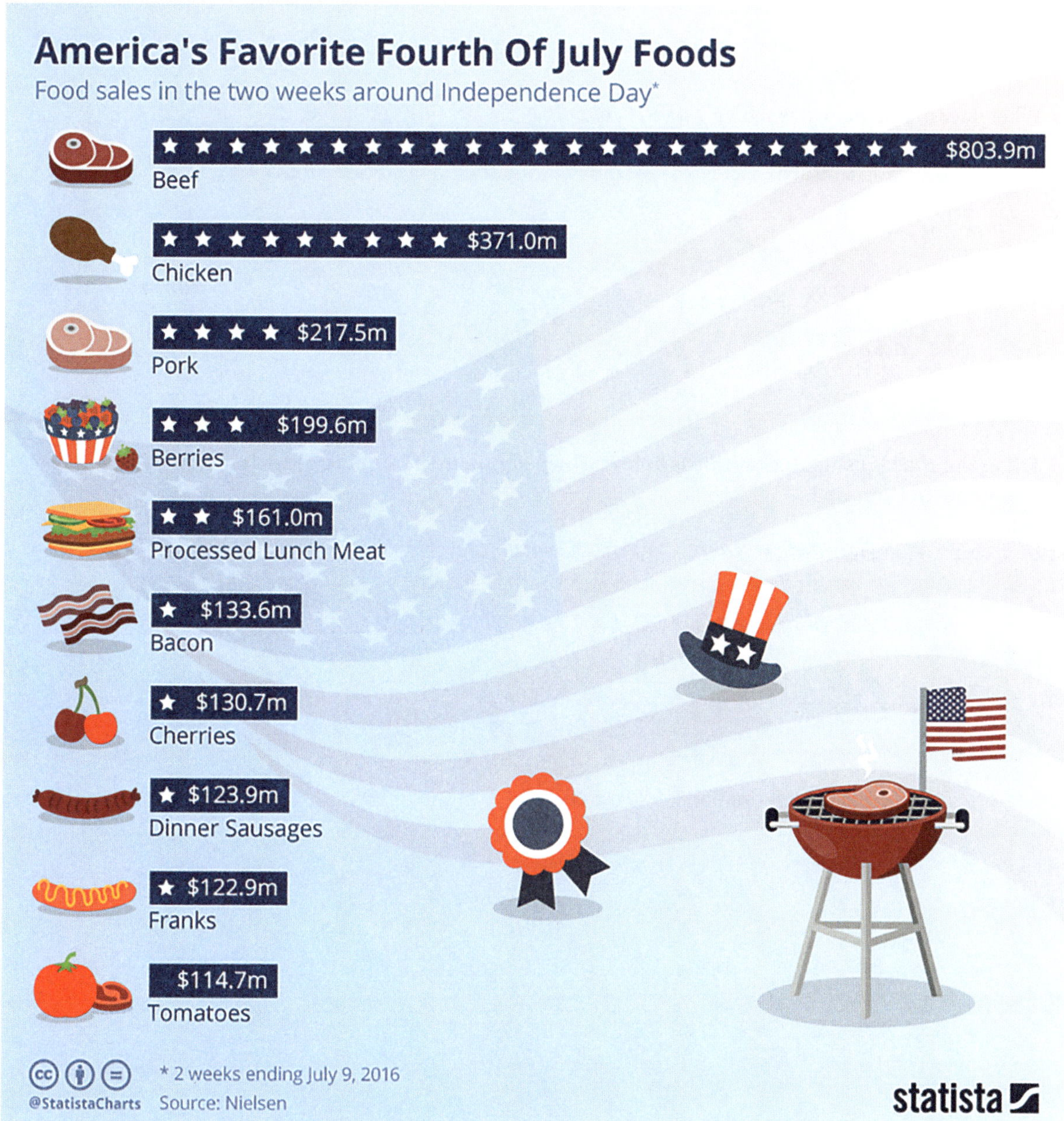

Fourth of July/Independence Day amerikanischer Unabhängigkeitstag — **m** h.: Million — **berry** Beere — **processed lunch meat** industriell verarbeiteter Aufschnitt — **cherry** Kirsche — **dinner sausage** Würstchen — **frank** Hotdog

*The Statista bar chart uses the American spelling: **favorite**.
We use the British spelling: **favourite.**

Step 1 Basic information

1. **Fill in the missing information. You do not need to write complete sentences. The sample bar chart and information on page 4 can help you.**

a) What is the **title** of the bar chart? ....

b) What is the **source** of the information in the bar chart? ....

c) What **type** of bar chart is it? ....

d) What does the **vertical axis** show? Ten different ....

e) What does the **horizontal axis** show? *(This information should include the units.)*

Millions of ....

f) What does each **bar** show? .... sales in .... dollars for the

two weeks ending ....

2. **Fill in the spaces using the keywords below. Then complete the sentences with the information you wrote in exercise 1.**

axis • bar • horizontal • source • title • bar chart

a) The ________ of this bar chart is ....

....

b) The ________ of the information in the bar chart is ....

c) It is a .... type of ________ .

d) The vertical ________ shows ....

....

e) The ________ axis shows ....

f) Each ________ shows ....

....

Step 2 Description and analysis of the bar chart and data

3. Complete the description with the missing numbers.

The data shows that beef had the highest ($.................... m) amount in sales. It sold more than twice as much as chicken, which is the next food on the list. Americans paid less ($.................... m) for tomatoes than any other food on the list. Of the .... foods, ... are types of meat.

4. What does the bar chart tell you? Mark the correct answer.

- ◌ Beef tastes better than tomatoes.
- ◌ Americans spend more money on meat than on fruits and vegetables.
- ◌ Americans eat more meat than fruits and vegetables.
- ◌ Vegetarians do not celebrate the Fourth of July.

5. Complete the sentences. The first letters of the missing words or phrases are given.

Americans obviously eat a lot of meat on the F...................................... However, meat is usually more expensive than f...................................... and v...................................... It is possible that Americans just spend more money on expensive m.................... than on inexp...................................... fruit and vegetables.

Step 3 Evaluation: Your opinion

Write an evaluation of the data. These questions may help you.

— What did you find especially interesting or surprising about the data?

— What other data about this topic would be helpful or interesting?

....

....

....

....

....

....

....

....

....

BAR CHART 2

Semi-guided

The UK's Housework Gender Roles

UK / Gender roles

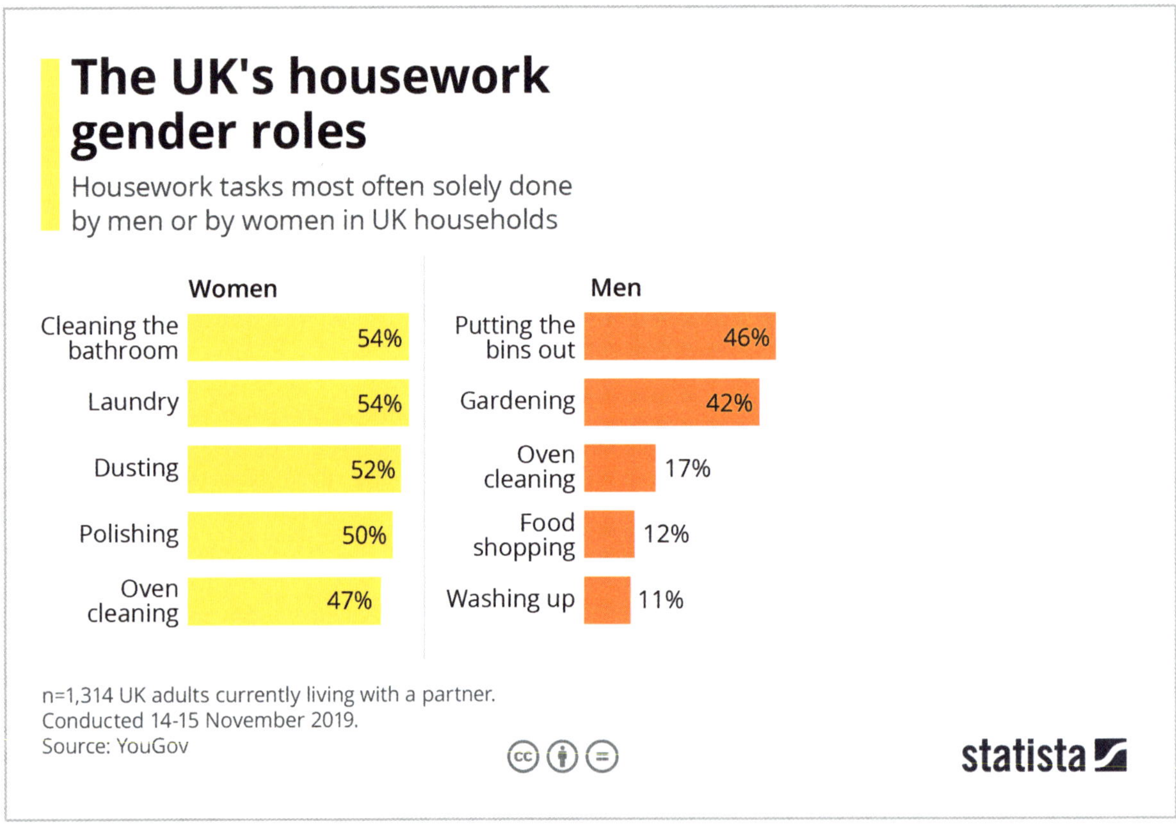

gender Geschlecht — **role** Rolle — **task** Aufgabe — **solely** allein — **laundry** Wäsche — **dusting** Staubwischen — **polishing** Polieren — **currently** aktuell — **n** h.: Anzahl der befragten Personen — **to survey** befragen — **percentage** Prozentsatz — **equality** Gleichberechtigung

Step 1 Basic information

1. Complete the sentences.

The title of these two bar charts is ....

....

....

They are .... (simple/multiple) bar charts. The source is ....

...., which surveyed ....

.... on ....

2. Use the correct forms of the words to write a sentence describing each axis.

vertical axis • of each chart • show • five • different • housework task

....

....

horizontal axis • show • men/women • percentage

....

....

3. Put the parts of the two sentences in the correct order. Then write the sentences.

◯ are orange.
◯ the percentage of women/men
◯ the bars for men
◯ are yellow
◯ Each bar shows
◯ and
◯ who do that task solely.
(1) The bars for women

....

....

....

....

Step 2 Description and analysis of the bar chart and data

4. Complete the text with the right words from the table below.

The data shows that women solely do a (1) .... percentage of housework tasks than men. Women do (2) .... 54% (cleaning the bathroom) and 47% (oven cleaning) of these housework tasks by themselves.

The greatest (3) .... in the tasks done solely by men is 46% (putting the bins out); the smallest is (4) .... 11% (washing up).

(5) .... all of the tasks done only by women are in the (6) ...., three out of the five tasks only done by men take place outside the house (putting the bins out, (7) ...., and food shopping).

1	greater	better	tinier
2	about	more than	between
3	percentage	amount	number
4	at least	just	around
5	While	Whether	Either
6	survey	day	house
7	gardening	oven cleaning	washing up

Step 3 Evaluation: Your opinion

Write an evaluation of the data. These questions may help you.

— Does the data surprise you?

— What do you think the data says about gender equality?

BAR CHART 3

Your turn

7 in 10 American Teens Use TikTok

US / Social media

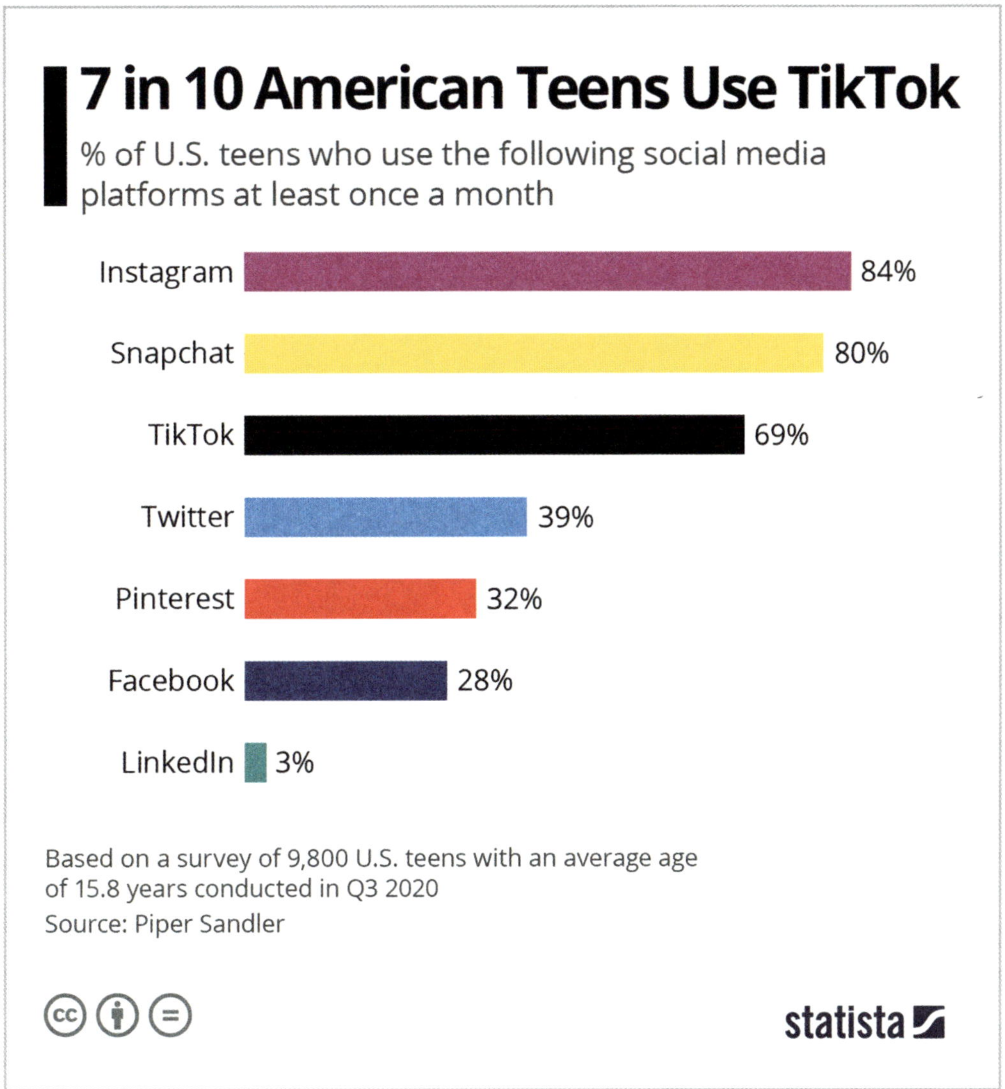

to conduct a survey eine Umfrage durchführen — **to survey** befragen — **percentage** Prozentsatz — **to add up to** zusammen ergeben

Describe and analyse the chart. Use a separate sheet of paper.

TIP

For your evaluation, think about how this chart compares with your own use of social media.

LINE CHARTS

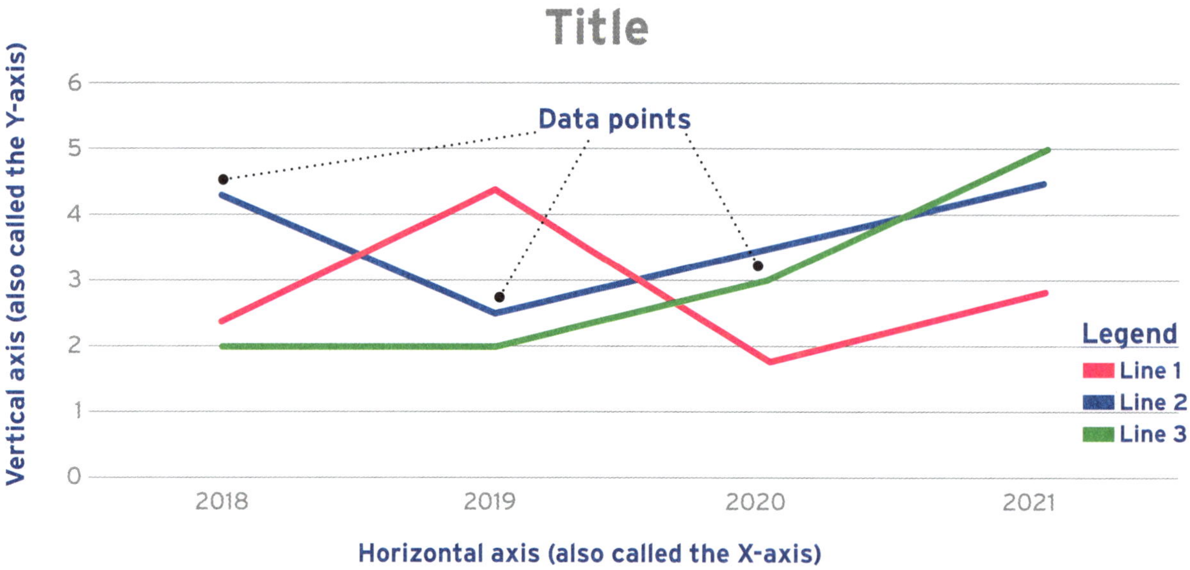

FACT FILE

A line chart shows a trend, change, or development in data over a period of time. It can have one or more lines.

Look at the scale of a line graph carefully. Where does it start and end? Scales that don't begin at zero can make small differences look bigger.

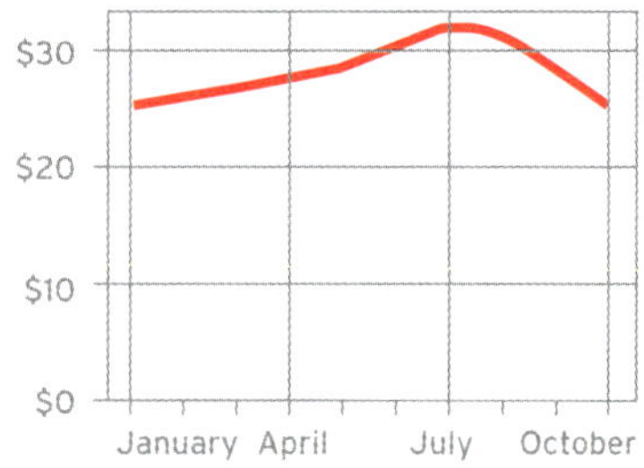

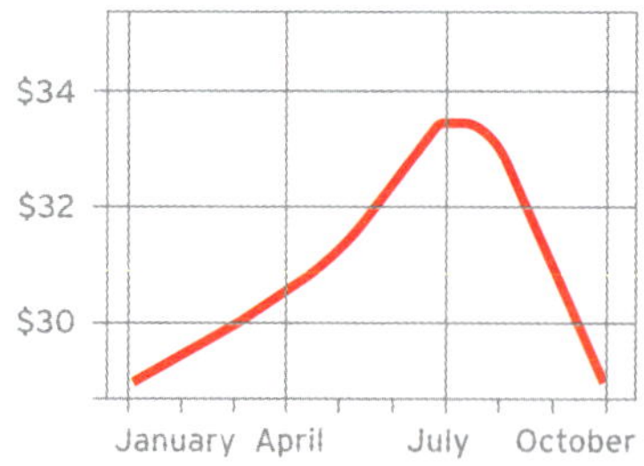

The scale on the left starts at 0, the scale on the right at $30. The data is the same.

chart Diagramm — **data** Daten — **scale** Skala — **unit** Einheit — **steadily** stetig; kontinuierlich — **significantly** bedeutend

GUIDELINES FOR DESCRIBING AND ANALYSING A LINE CHART

— What does each axis show?

a) What are the units (time, number of people or things, money, etc.)?

b) What is the scale (for example, from when to when does the axis go)?

The vertical axis (Y-axis) shows the number / percentage (%) / amount of … on a scale of … to … .
The horizontal axis (X-axis) is a timeline from … to …

— What does each line show? If there are several lines, how does each one look (red, dotted, etc.)?

The … line shows …

— What does the data show? What is the general trend? What is the most meaningful data?

The data shows that the number of … increased / rose / fell / stayed the same / decreased / dropped (slowly / quickly / steadily / steeply / greatly / significantly / a little bit) between … and … / from … to … / until …
The largest / smallest number of … was in … The greatest increase / decline was from … to …

LINE CHART 1

Guided

US Cases Drop as Europe Faces Third Wave

US / EU / The coronavirus pandemic

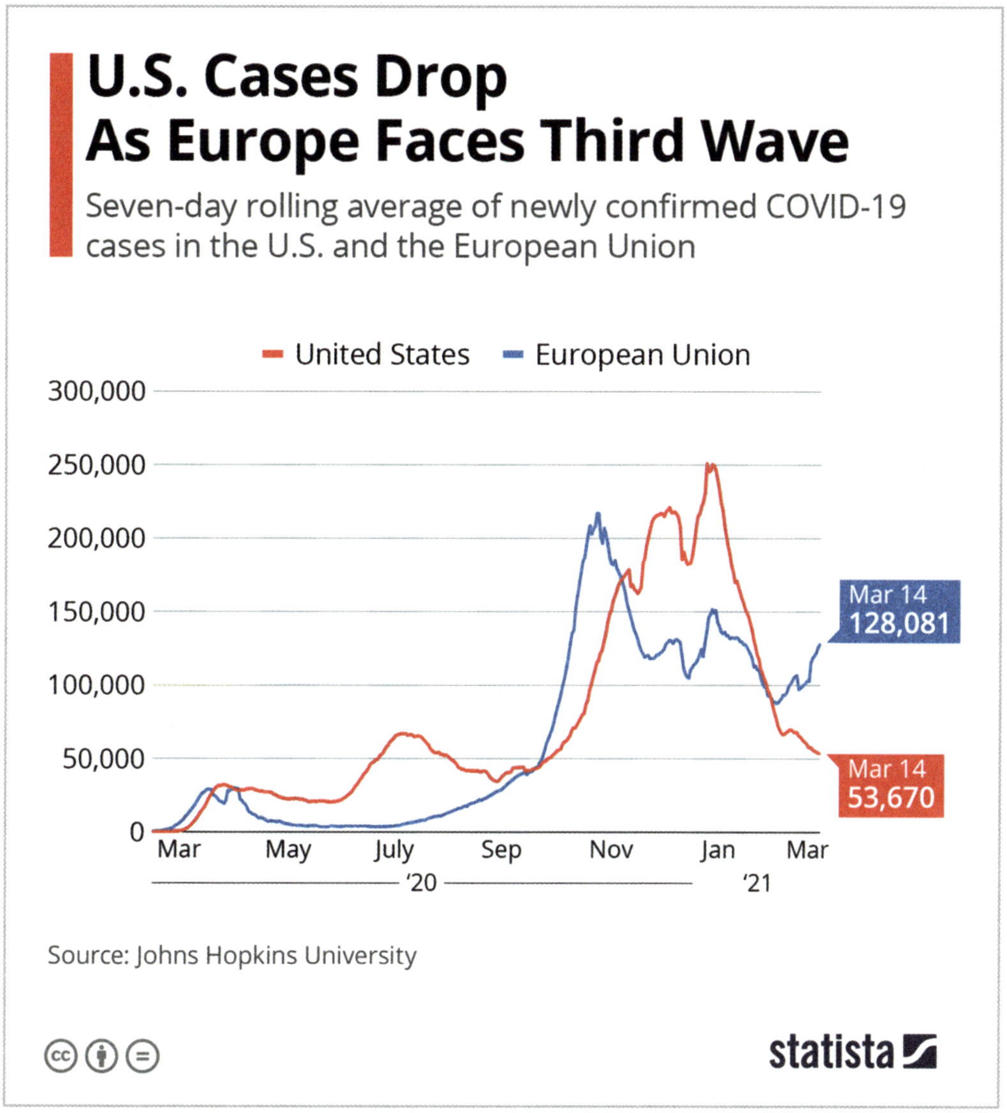

rolling average gleitender Durchschnitt — **to confirm** bestätigen — **case** Fall

Step 1 Basic information

1. **Fill in the missing information. You do not need to write complete sentences. The sample line chart and information on page 12 can help you.**

a) What is the **title** of the line chart?

....

....

....

....

b) What is the **source** of the data in the line chart?

....

c) What does the **vertical axis** show? *(This information should include the scale.)*

....

....

d) What does the **horizontal axis** show?

....

e) What does the **red line** show?

....

....

f) What does the **blue line** show?

....

....

Step 2 Description and analysis of the line chart and data

2. **Complete the description with verbs and adverbs. Make sure to use the correct form of each verb.**

be • fall • pass • reach • rise • start off • stay at

downwards • fairly • quickly • steeply • upwards

The data shows that both the US and EU __________ with about zero cases in March 2020. The number of cases rose a little more __________ in the EU than in the US. Both the US and EU __________ about 30,000 cases at the end of March. In the EU, the number of cases began to ______ at the beginning of April. By the middle of May 2020, the number of new cases dropped to only a few thousand per week in the EU. The number of cases in the US ______ about 20,000–25,000 until the middle of June, when it began to rise ______ again. Numbers in the EU stayed ______ low, but they began to ______ sharply in late summer and early autumn. The number of cases in the EU ______ the number in the US at the beginning of October. After early November, the general trend was ______ in the EU but ______ in the US. In January 2021, the number of cases ______ around 250,000 in the US and 150,000 in the EU. By March 2021, the EU had more than twice as many COVID cases as the US.

Step 3 Evaluation: Your opinion

Write an evaluation of the data. These questions may help you.

— What did you find interesting or surprising about the data?

— What factors might explain the trends in the data?

LINE CHART 2

Semi-guided

The Steady Rise of Podcasts

US / Media and technology

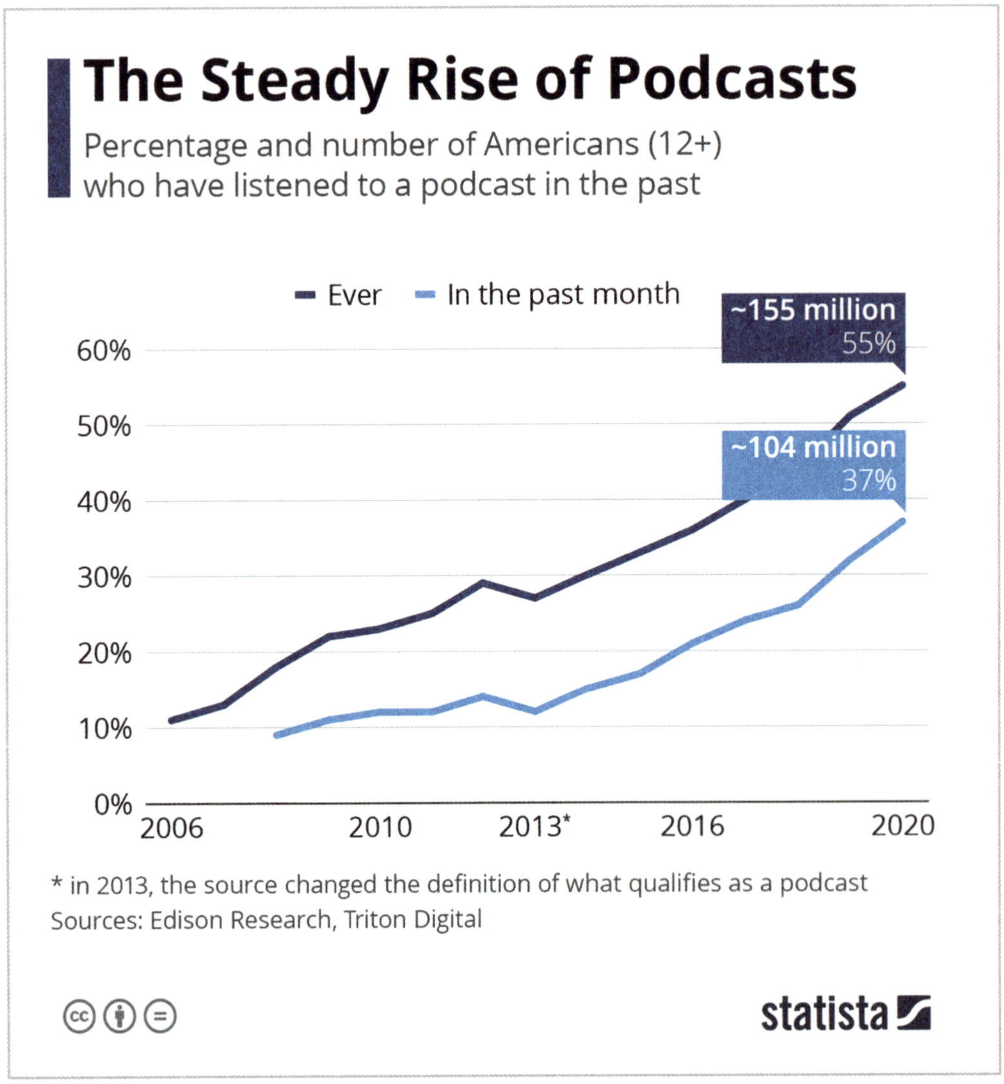

steady stetig; gleichmäßig — **rise** Anstieg; Zunahme — **percentage** Prozentsatz — **to qualify as s.th.** h.: als etw. zählen — **dip** Senkung

Step 1 Basic information

1. Complete the sentences.

The title ....

....

....

....

The sources of the data are .... and

....

The vertical axis shows ....

....

on a scale of ....

The horizontal axis is a timeline of ....

The dark blue line ....

....

The .... line shows ....

....

....

Step 2 Description and analysis of the line chart and data

2. What does a first look at the line chart tell you?

- ◌ The number of Americans who have listened to a podcast is rising.
- ◌ Millions of Americans regularly listen to podcasts.
- ◌ Podcasts were popular between 2006 and 2020.

3. Write two sentences to describe the change in each line from 2006 to 2020. Use these building blocks. You need two building blocks once, the others twice.

in 2020.

The percentage of Americans

to about .... (around .... million people)

who had ever listened to a podcast

rose from about .... % in ....

who had listened to a podcast in the past month

4. **Complete the sentences with information from the chart.**

As the title of the line chart says, the data shows a …………………………………………………… of podcasts. However, there was a small dip in …………………… . The information in the footnote for that year explains this dip. It says that 'the source changed ……'. It seems that the change meant that fewer programmes qualified as ……………………………………………: that led to a dip in the numbers.

Step 3 Evaluation: Your opinion

Write an evaluation of the data. These questions may help you.

— What do you think is especially interesting?

— What else would you like to know?

— How do you think these numbers changed after the line chart was created? Do you think they have gone up or down? Why?

LINE CHART 3

Your turn

Number of Kids per Household on Decline

Australia / Society

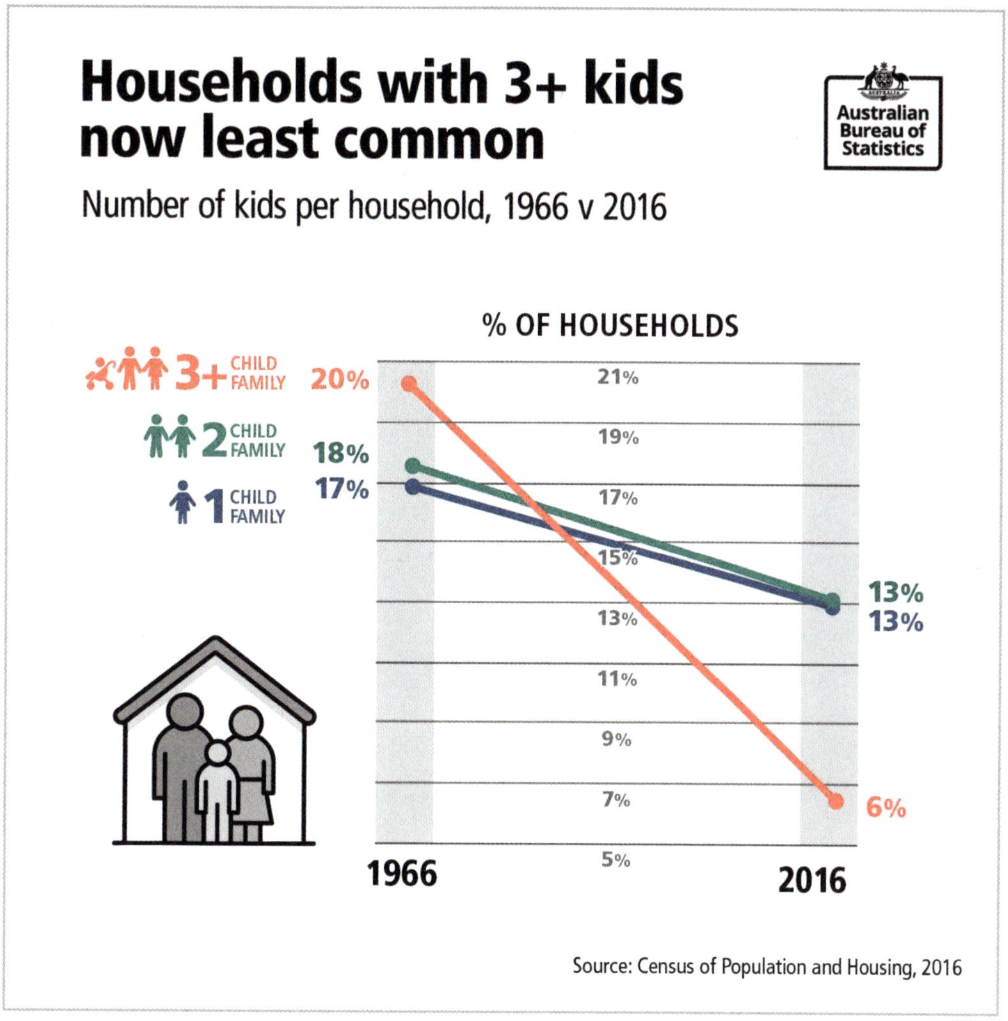

household Haushalt — **to be on (the) decline; decline** abnehmen, zurückgehen; Rückgang — **resident** Bewohner(in) — **census** Volkszählung — **percentage** (prozentualer) Anteil

Describe and analyse the chart. Use a separate sheet of paper.

PIE CHARTS

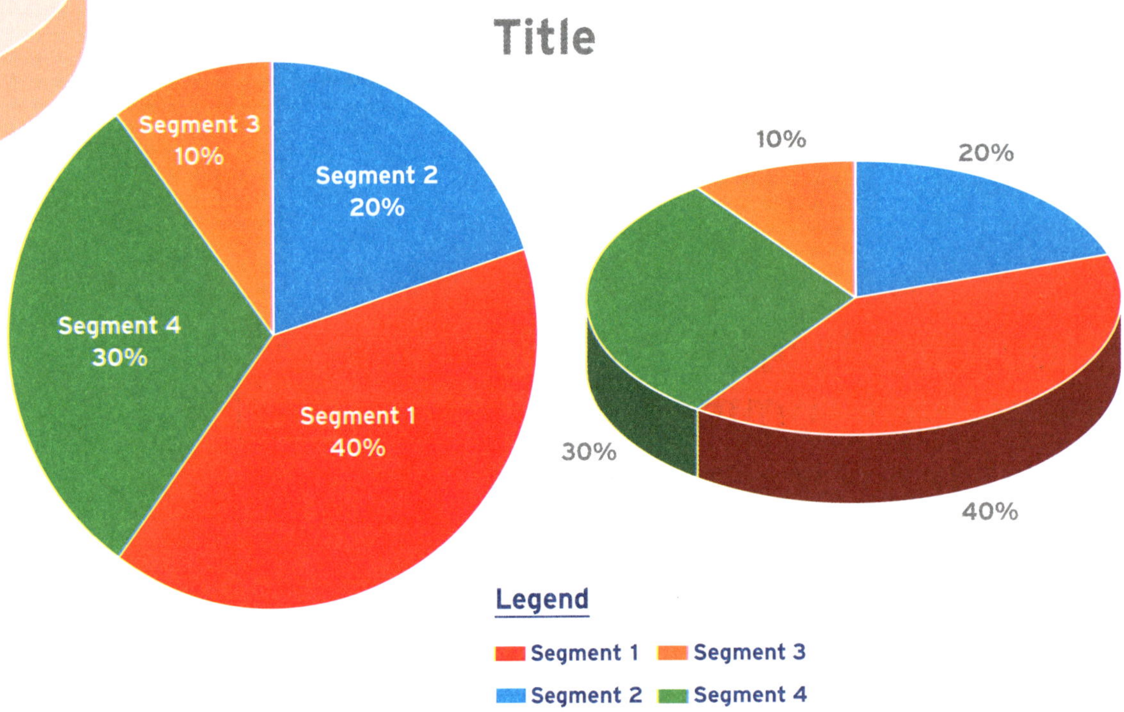

FACT FILE

A pie chart shows the size, usually in percentages, of each different part of one thing. The segments of the pie add up to 100% of that thing.

— Pie charts are often used to show the results of a survey. Each person usually gives one answer to one question.

— The size of each segment of a pie chart corresponds to its value as part of the whole. If a segment represents 50% of the whole, then the size of that segment will be half of the pie.

— Sometimes only one segment is important. This segment may be shown outside of the pie (an 'exploded' pie chart) or may have a special colour.

— In some pie charts, the description and size is on each segment. This can be hard to read when there are many small segments. The name or size of small segments are next to it or in a legend.

pie Kuchen; Torte — **chart** Diagramm — **segment** Teilstück — **legend** Legende — **to add up to** zusammen ergeben — **survey** Umfrage — **to correspond to** entsprechen — **to represent** darstellen

GUIDELINES FOR DESCRIBING AND ANALYSING A PIE CHART

— What does the pie chart look like? What does each segment show?

The pie chart has … (different coloured) segments.
Each segment shows …

— What does the data show?

The pie shows that … was the most popular / common / …

Almost / About / More than / Less than / Only / … half / one quarter / three quarters / two thirds / a tenth / 20% / one in five …

PIE CHART 1

Guided

Fewer Americans Are Driving to Work

US / Transportation / Work / Environment

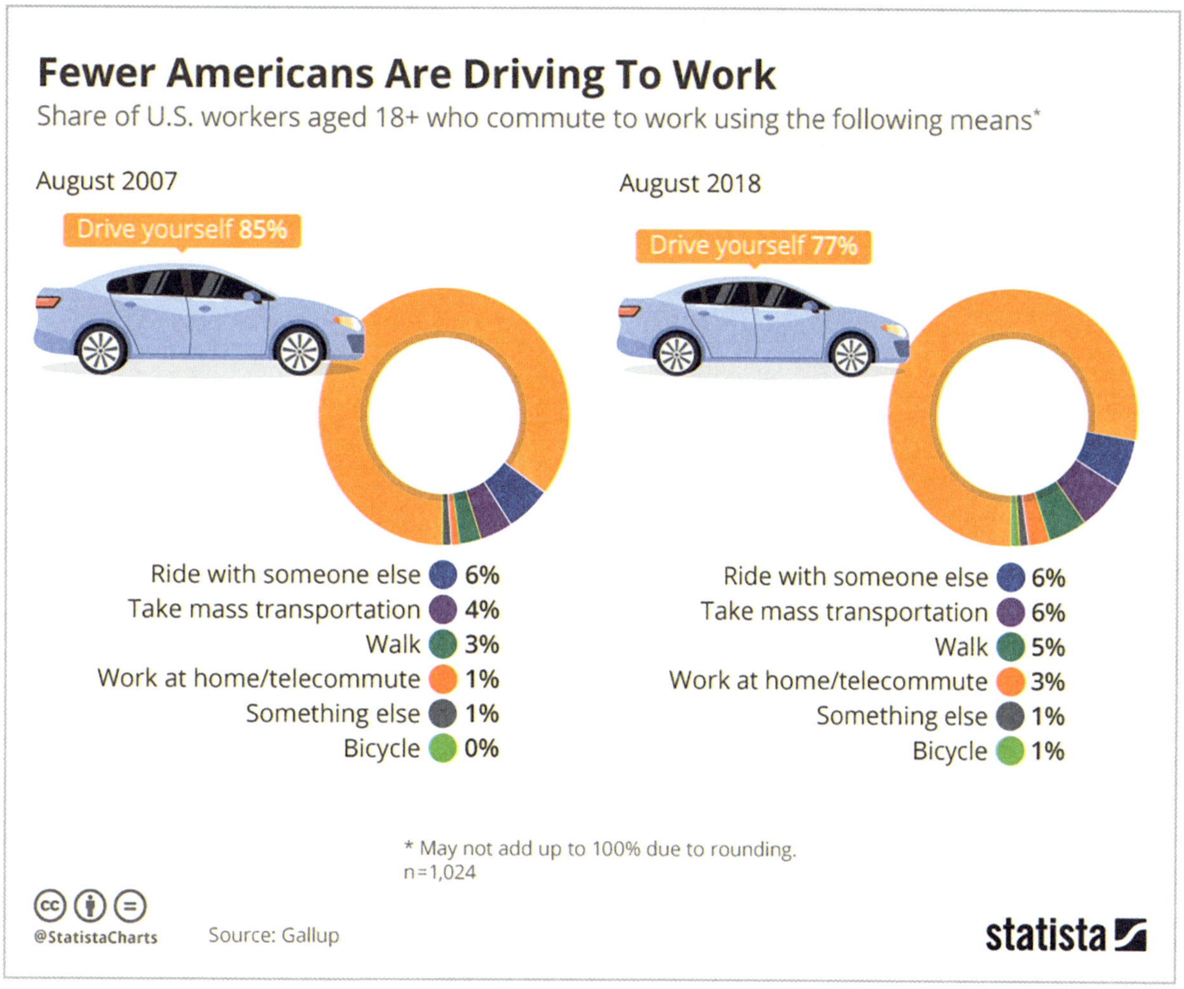

to commute pendeln — **means (of transportation)** h.: Transportmittel — **to drive yourself** selbst fahren — **mass transportation** ÖPNV — **to telecommute** Telearbeit machen — **rounding** Aufrunden — **n** h.: Anzahl der befragten Personen — **to survey** befragen — **caption** Beschriftung

Step 1 Basic information

1. **Fill in the missing information. You do not need to write complete sentences. The sample pie chart and information on page 20 can help you.**

a) What is the **title** of the pie charts?

....

....

b) What is the **source** of the data in the pie charts? ....

c) How many people were **surveyed**? ....

d) What is the **caption** of the pie chart **on the left**? ....

e) What is the **caption** of the pie chart **on the right**? ....

f) What do the pie charts **look like**? *(This information should include the number of segments.)*

....

g) What does each **segment** show?

....

h) What information is in the **legend**?

....

....

Step 2 Description and analysis of the pie charts and data

2. **Write the information.**

2007

a) Most popular way to get to work?..

b) Percentage of people? ....

c) Least popular way to get to work?..

d) Percentage of people? ....

2018

e) Most popular way to get to work?

f) Percentage of people?

g) Least popular way to get to work?

h) Percentage of people?

3. **Which statement best summarises the data? Mark the correct answer.**

- A car is the best way to commute to work in the US.
- Although the percentage fell from 2007, most American workers still commuted by car in 2018.
- Environmentally friendly means of transportation were much more popular in 2018 than in 2007.
- Many people use several different means of transportation.

Step 3 Evaluation: Your opinion

Write an evaluation of the data. These questions may help you.

— What did you find especially interesting or surprising about the data?

— How do you think this data compares with Germany's?

— How do you think these numbers have developed since August 2018?

— How do you think these numbers change in different seasons?

PIE CHART 2

Semi-guided

Do Brits Miss Going to the Pub?

UK / Culture / The coronavirus pandemic

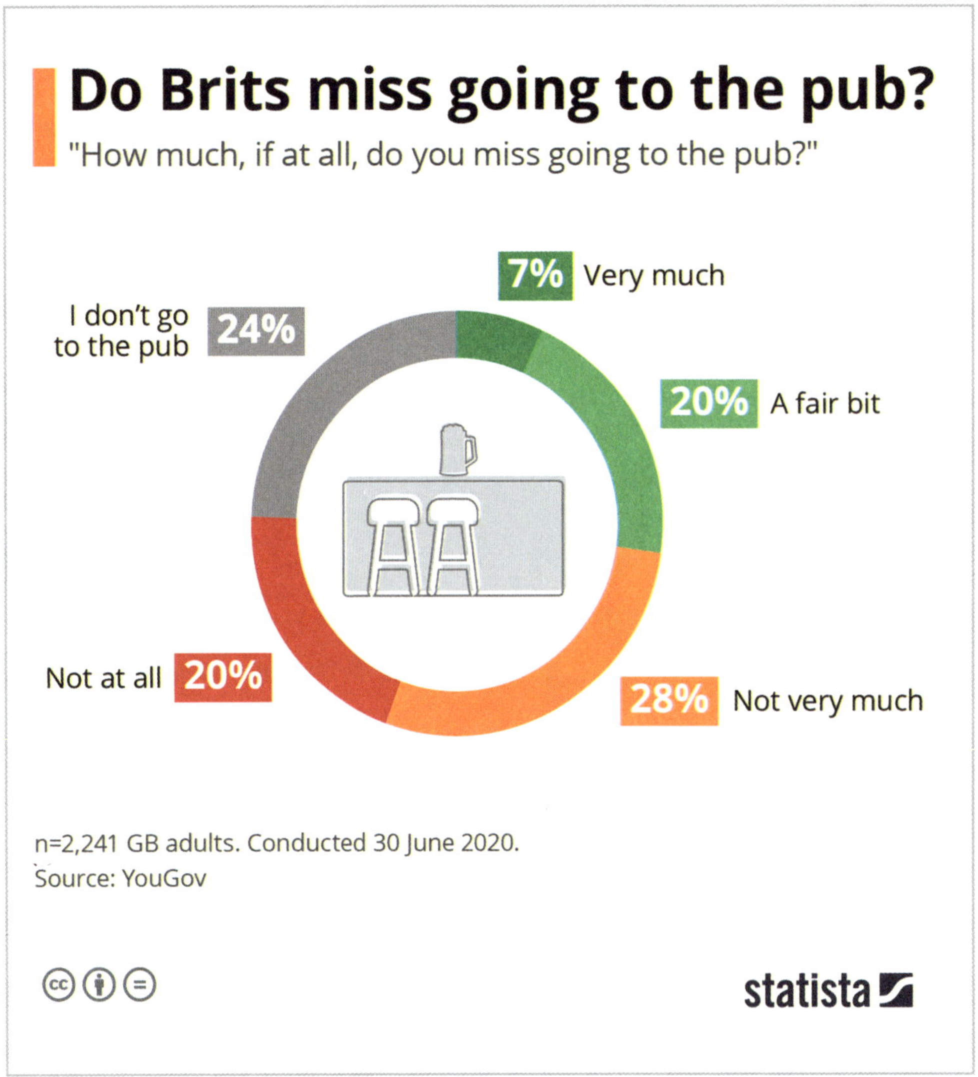

Brit Brite(-in) — **pub** Kneipe — **if at all** wenn überhaupt — **a fair bit** ziemlich — **to conduct** durchführen — **pandemic** Pandemie — **to survey** befragen

Step 1 Basic information

1. **Complete the sentences.**

The title of this pie chart is ....

....

The source of the information is.., which surveyed ....

....

.... on .... The pie chart has .... segments.

2. **Put the parts of the sentence in the right order. Then write the sentence.**

- ◌ shows
- ◌ and the percentage of Britons
- ◌ Each segment
- ◌ the question in the title
- ◌ who gave that answer.
- ◌ a different answer to

TIP

The punctuation and big and small letters will help you put the parts of the sentence in the right order.

....

....

Step 2 Description and analysis of the pie chart and data

3. **Answer the questions in complete sentences.**

a) What important world event was happening in June 2020?

....

....

b) Why didn't people go to the pub during this event? Name two reasons.

....

....

c) What are the largest and smallest segments of the pie chart?

....

....

d) Many people think pubs are an important part of British life. Does the information in the pie chart support this idea? Give evidence.

Step 3 Evaluation: Your opinion

Write an evaluation of the data. These questions may help you.

— Does the data surprise you?

— How do you think Britons would have answered this question later in the pandemic?

— What other factors might change how people answered the question?

PIE CHART 3

Your turn

Women Are an Endangered Species in Hollywood

US / Gender / Culture

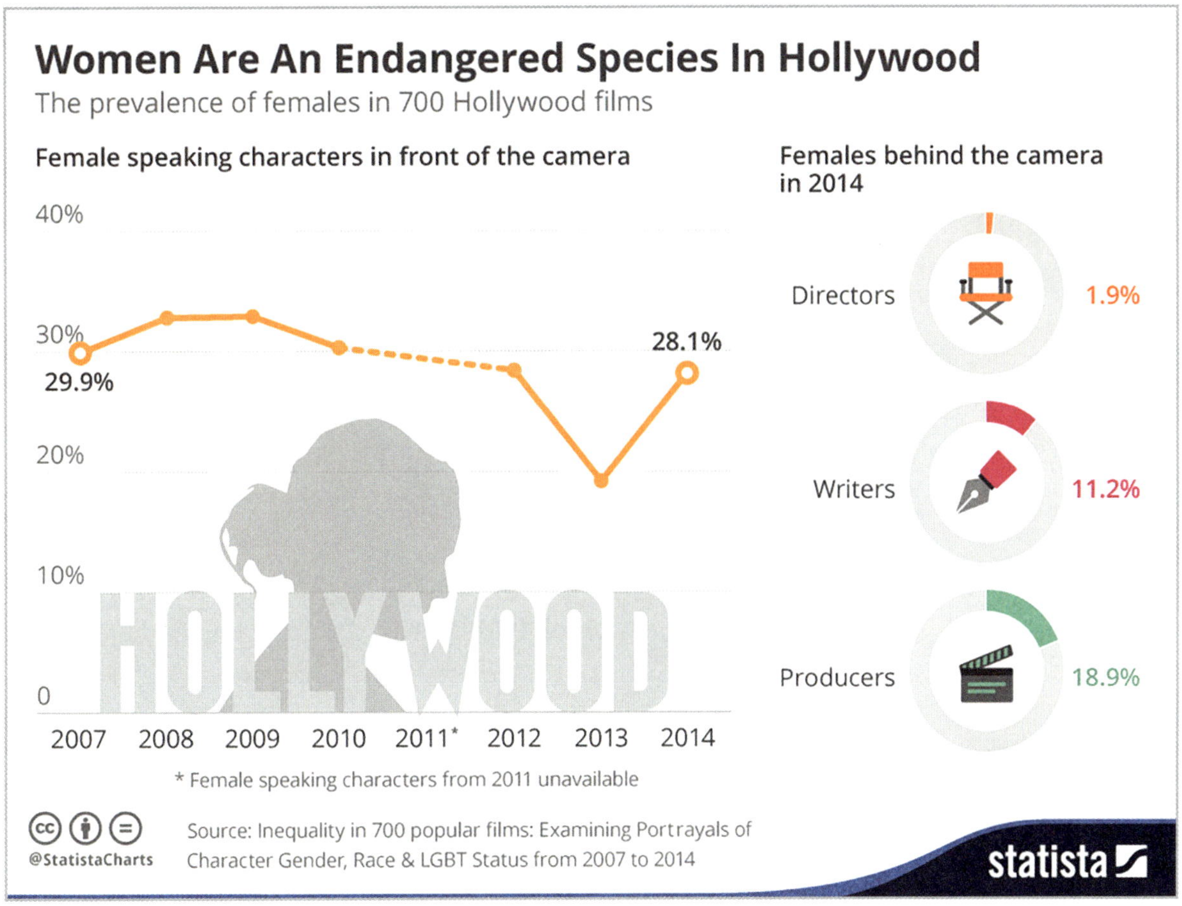

endangered gefährdet — **species** Spezies; **to be an endangered species** eine vom Aussterben bedrohte Art sein — **director** Regisseur(in) — **producer** Produzent(in) — **inequality** Ungleichheit — **to examine** untersuchen — **portrayal** Darstellung — **gender** Geschlecht — **race** Herkunft — **LGBT = lesbian, gay, bisexual, and transgender** Lesben, Schwule, Bisexuelle und Transgender

Describe and analyse the pie charts on the right. Use a separate sheet of paper.

MAPS

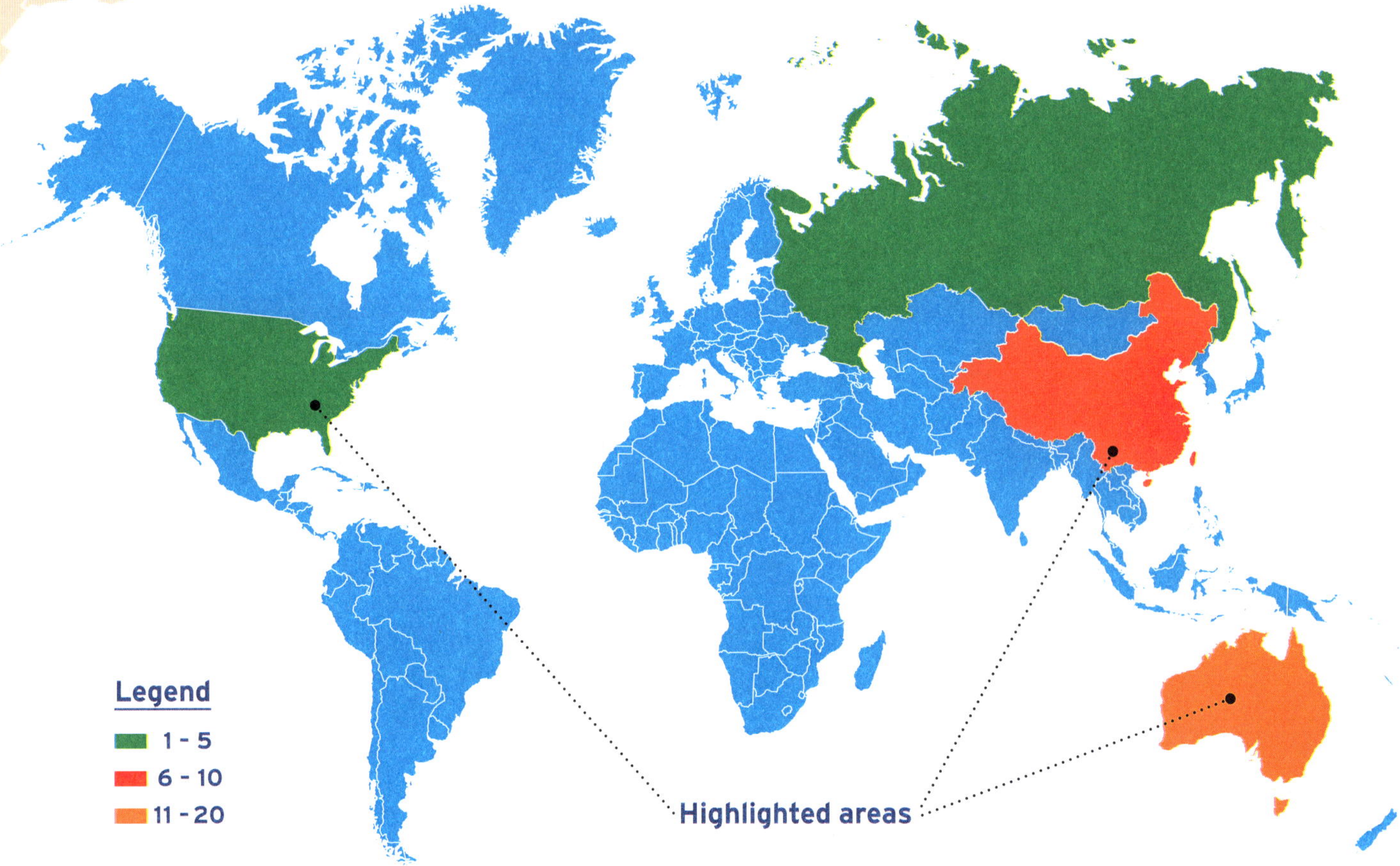

FACT FILE

A map is a drawing that shows part or all of the world or universe, buildings, or other places. Maps may show political borders, geographical features, roads, etc. Maps can be graphs when they show statistics about certain areas.

to highlight hervorheben — **geographical feature** landschaftliche Gegebenheit — **graph** Diagramm; Schaubild

GUIDELINES FOR DESCRIBING AND ANALYSING A MAP

— What area does the map show?
The map is of the world / Europe / New York / ….

— What does the map look like?
The colour of each country on the map corresponds to …

— What information does the map contain? How is this information shown on the map?
Countries that … are shown in … / The names of … are written on the map.

MAP 1

Guided

Hardest Hit by Extreme Weather Conditions

World / Environment

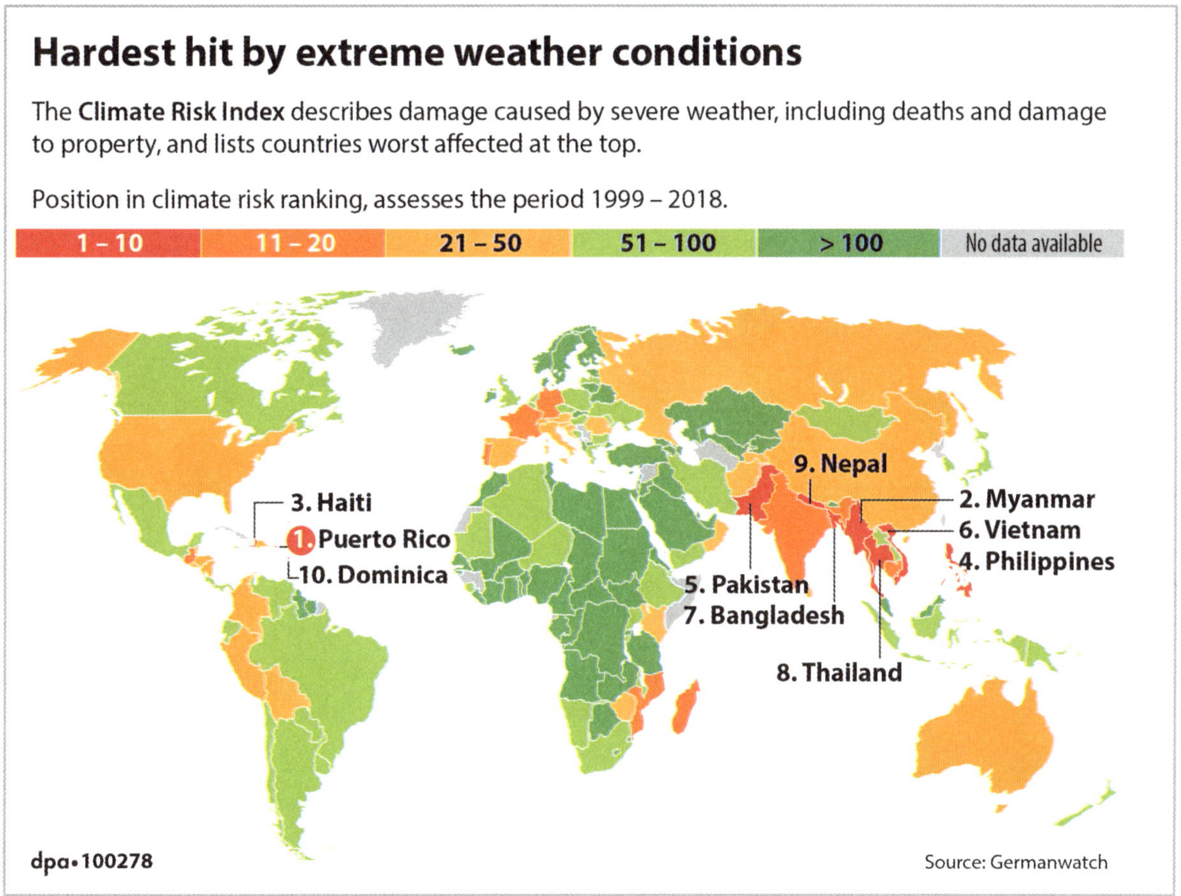

to hit; s.w.u. **to affect** betreffen — **risk** Risiko — **to cause** verursachen — **severe weather** Unwetter — **ranking** Rangliste — **to assess** auswerten — **data** Daten — **to correspond to** entsprechen — **particular** einzeln — **territory** Hoheitsgebiet — **to divide** aufteilen — **geographic** geografisch — **criterion** Kriterium

Step 1 Basic information

1. **Fill in the missing information. You do not need to write complete sentences. The sample map and information on page 28 can help you.**

a) What is the title of the map? *(Don't include a subtitle.)* ....

....

b) What is the source of the map? ....

c) What area does the map show? ....

d) What period of time is shown? ....

Step 2 Description and analysis of the map and data

2. Look at the text. Five parts are missing. Choose the correct gap (1–7) in the text for each of the parts below (A–E). Write the correct number of each gap in the circle on the left. There are two gaps which you do not need to use.

The colour of each country on the map corresponds to its position in the climate risk ranking. (1)
The ten worst affected countries are red, and their names are on the map. (2) For a few countries, there is no data available, so (3).
The top country in the ranking is Puerto Rico. There are two other top-ten countries near Puerto Rico, (4).
Germany is orange and in the 11th–20th position. The US is yellow and in the 21st–50th position, while (5).
Although the number-one country in the ranking is in the Americas, the riskiest area is Asia:
seven of the top-ten countries are there. (6) Africa is the safest area on the map: almost all of it is dark or light green (positions 51 plus). (7)

- A but the rest are in Asia.
- B the UK is green (51st–100th position).
- C The next ten countries in the ranking are orange, etc.
- D There is also a lot of orange and yellow in Asia.
- E these countries are grey.

Step 3 Evaluation: Your opinion

Write an evaluation of the data. These questions may help you.

— What do you notice about the time period shown?

— What do you find especially interesting or surprising about the data?

— What additional information would you be interested in seeing?

— The data is shown by country. In what other way could it be shown? How might the map look then?

MAP 2

Semi-guided

The US Has the Highest Share of Single Parenting

World / Society

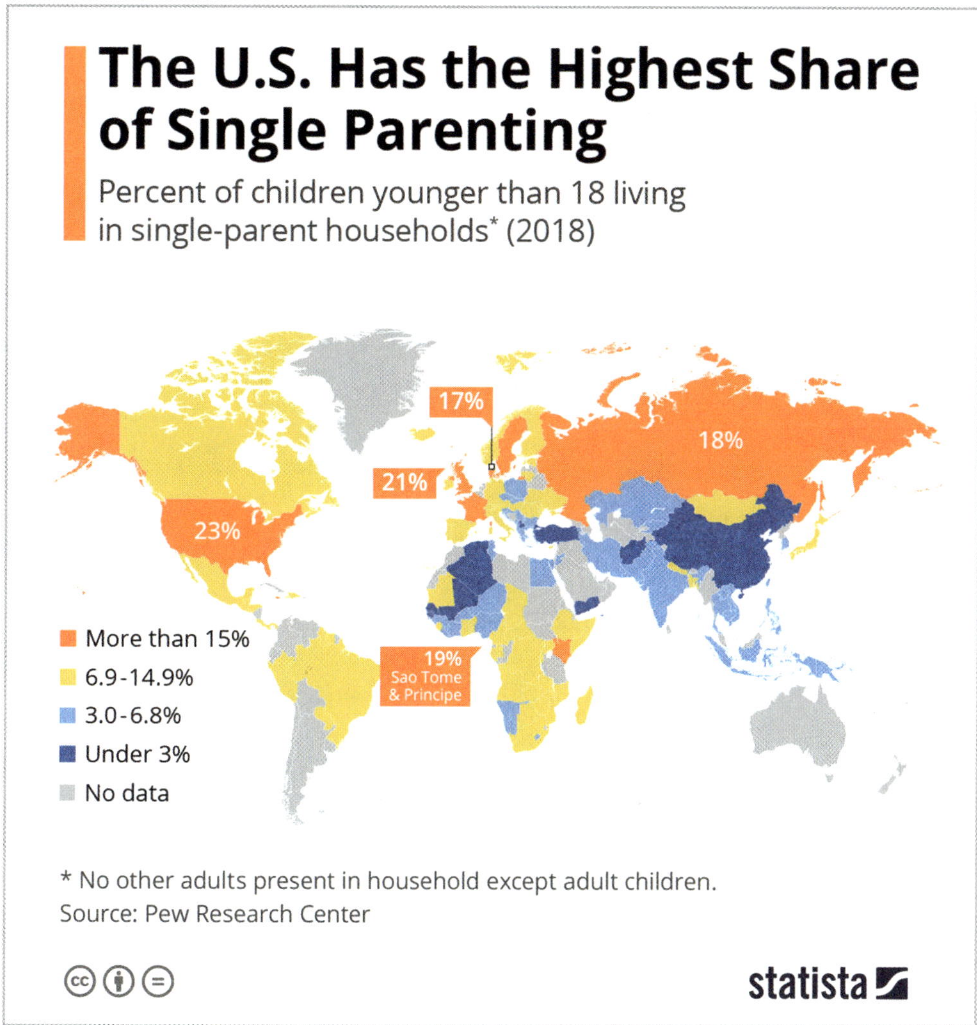

share Anteil — **household** Haushalt — **to correspond to** entsprechen — **percentage** Prozentsatz; Anteil

Step 1 Basic information

1. **Write a short introduction. Include the title and source of the map.**

Step 2 Description and analysis of the map and data

2. **Use phrases from the box to complete the text. Capitalise the phrases if you use them at the beginning of a sentence.**

6.9% • 14.9% • a low share of single parenting • are yellow and orange • belong to this group • corresponds to the percentage • exact percentages • the highest percentage of single-parent households • in the legend • is close behind with 21% • is in the yellow group • light and dark blue • may be less common • may be more likely • more than 15% • These countries are grey • without any data available

TIP
Before you try to match the phrases in the box with the gaps, read each sentence. Think about what kind of phrase would fit in the gap(s). Then look for a similar phrase in the box above.

The colour of each country in the map .... of its children living in single-parent households. The meaning of each colour is given .... The countries with .... of children in this situation are orange. The .... of several of them are written on the map. The next group (...) is yellow and so on. For a few countries, there is no data available. .... As the title of the map says, the US has .... (23%). The UK .... Germany .... Large parts of Africa, the Middle East, and Asia are .... They are the lowest groups for which there is information. Most of the Americas and Europe .... They are the two highest groups. The countries .... are mostly in South America, Africa, and the Middle East. Australia and some Pacific island nations also .... Many of the countries that show .... on the map are places where religion plays a large role: divorce and having children without being married .... in these countries. Several generations .... to live together.

Step 3 Evaluation: Your opinion

Write an evaluation of the data. These questions may help you.

— How would you define 'single-parent household'? Is it the same as the definition used for the map?

— Is there anything about the data that surprised you? Think about the colours of different countries on the map. What do the colours say about the countries?

MAP 3

Your turn

The Countries Banning Plastic Bags

World / Environment / Business

ban Verbot — **to ban** verbieten — **level** Ebene — **regulation** Verordnung; Gesetz — **partial** Teil- — **to be under consideration** zur Diskussion stehen — **to be in effect** in Kraft sein — **United Nations** Vereinte Nationen

Describe and analyse the map. Use a separate sheet of paper.

TIP

Which countries have you been in? Do the colours on the map match your observations and experiences in those countries?

TABLES

	Heading column 1	Heading column 2	Heading column 3
Row 1	data	data	data
Row 2	data	data	data
Row 3	data	data	data
Row 4	data	data	data

FACT FILE

A table presents data or information in **columns** and **rows**. Headings at the top and on the left tell you what information is in each column or row. Sometimes they also give you the unit of measurement.

— The data in tables can be numbers, text, symbols, or other types of information. A table can also combine different types of information.

— Columns or rows with several subheadings may be grouped under one heading (see **Table 1**).

column Säule — **row** Reihe — **heading** Überschrift — **unit of measurement** Maßeinheit — **subheading** Unterüberschrift

GUIDELINES FOR DESCRIBING AND ANALYSING A TABLE

— What kind of table is it?
This is a simple/complex table (with many headings and subheadings).

— How many rows and columns are in the table?
There are … rows and … columns in the table./
The table has/contains … rows and … columns.

— What is in each column/row? What are the units (month/year, percentage, dollars, etc.)?
The columns/rows show years/names/the percentages of … /symbols …

TABLE 1

Guided

Number of Children and Poverty in American Families

US / Poverty / Families

Number of Children and Poverty

Male (Population in thousands)		Total	In families with no own children under 18 years	In families with one or more own children under 18 years	1 child	2 or more children	In families with one or more own children under 6 years	1 child	2 or more children
16 to 24 years	All income levels	15,891	8,024	7,866	4,059	3,807	1,077	858	219
	Below poverty line	1,258	486	772	323	450	220	159	61
	% below poverty line	7.9	6.1	9.8	7.9	11.8	20.4	18.5	28.0
25 to 34 years	All income levels	15,489	9,449	6,041	2,695	3,346	4,501	2,968	1,533
	Below poverty line	871	383	488	145	344	362	202	160
	% below poverty line	5.6	4.1	8.1	5.4	10.3	8.0	6.8	10.4
35 years and over	All income levels	65,687	44,314	21,374	8,477	12,896	7,384	5,293	2,090
	Below poverty line	3,186	1,962	1,225	398	827	508	360	148
	% below poverty line	4.9	4.4	5.7	4.7	6.4	6.9	6.8	7.1

Female (Population in thousands)		Total	In families with no own children under 18 years	In families with one or more own children under 18 years	1 child	2 or more children	In families with one or more own children under 6 years	1 child	2 or more children
16 to 24 years	All income levels	15,497	7,366	8,131	4,273	3,858	1,629	1,259	370
	Below poverty line	1,370	438	933	354	579	457	309	147
	% below poverty line	8.8	5.9	11.5	8.3	15.0	28.0	24.6	39.8
25 to 34 years	All income levels	16,487	7,136	9,351	3,654	5,697	6,869	4,606	2,263
	Below poverty line	1,940	340	1,600	439	1,161	1,130	725	405
	% below poverty line	11.8	4.8	17.1	12.0	20.4	16.4	15.7	17.9
35 years and over	All income levels	71,097	48,090	23,007	9,599	13,408	6,578	4,851	1,727
	Below poverty line	4,494	2,521	1,974	682	1,292	706	520	186
	% below poverty line	6.3	5.2	8.6	7.1	9.6	10.7	10.7	10.7

Source: US Census Bureau

poverty Armut — **poverty line** Armutsgrenze — **to live below the poverty line** unter der Armutsgrenze leben — **census** Volkszählung — **bureau** Amt — **population** Bevölkerung(szahl) — **survey** Umfrage — **percentage** Prozentsatz — **complex** Komplex — **to divide** teilen — **to be divided into s.th.** in etw. unterteilt sein — **correlation** Korrelation; Zusammenhang — **to tend to do s.th.** dazu neigen, etw. zu tun — **increase** Anstieg — **rate** Quote; Anteil — **pattern** Muster — **shocked** schockiert — **absolute numbers** absolute Zahlen

Step 1 Basic information

1. **Fill in the missing information. You do not need to write complete sentences. The sample table and information on page 35 can help you.**

a) What is the **title** of the table? ....

....

b) What is the **source** of the table? ....

c) What **kind of table** is it? ....

....

d) How many **rows** are in the table? ....

e) How many **columns** are in the table? ....

Step 2 Description and analysis of the table and data

2. **Write the missing letters and numbers.**

This table is in two parts: one for males and one for f_ _ _ _ _ _. Each half of the table has rows for three a_ _ groups: 16–24 years, 25–34 years, and 3_ years and above. Within each one, we see the total p_ _ _ _ _ _ _ _ _ in that group and their i_ _ _ _ _ levels. We also see the number and p_ _ _ _ _ _ _ _ _ of people in that group living below the p_ _ _ _ _ _ line.

The columns show the populations in groups by the number and age of children in the f_ _ _ _ _.

The data shows relationships between sex, number of c_ _ _ _ _ _ _, age, and income level.

Being a young parent of two or more y_ _ _ _ (under six years) children has a stronger correlation to poverty than any other factor: 2_% of men and almost 4_% of women in this group are poor.

Least likely to live in poverty are men and women 2_ to _4 years old with no children under 1_ years: only around 4% of this group are poor.

3. **Mark the four statements that the data shows are generally true.**

- ◯ Parents are more likely to live below the poverty line than people without children.
- ◯ More children means more money.
- ◯ Men are poorer than women.
- ◯ Younger people are more likely to live below the poverty line than older people.
- ◯ Parents are richer than people without children.
- ◯ Older people are poorer than younger people.
- ◯ Women are poorer than men.
- ◯ More children means less money.

Step 3 Evaluation: Your opinion

Write an evaluation of the data. These questions may help you.

— Was it easy for you to understand the table and the data? Why or why not?

— What information in this table surprised you the most? Why?

— What conclusion about child poverty can you draw from this data?

— What other information about poverty would you be interested in seeing?

TABLE 2

Semi-guided

Countries and Regions by Life Expectancy at Birth in 2019

World / Health

Step 1 Basic information

1. **Write a short introduction that gives the title and source of the table.**

Countries and Regions by Life Expectancy at Birth in 2019 (2020 Report)

	Countries and regions	Life expectancy at birth: All	M	F	Gender life gap
1	Hong Kong	84.9	82.0	87.7	5.7
2	Japan	84.6	81.5	87.7	6.2
3	Switzerland	83.8	81.9	85.6	3.7
4	Singapore	83.6	81.5	85.7	4.2
5	Spain	83.5	80.8	86.2	5.4
6	Italy	83.4	81.3	85.5	4.2
7	Australia	83.4	81.5	85.4	3.9
8	Iceland	83.0	81.5	84.5	3.0
9	Israel	83.0	81.3	84.5	3.2
10	South Korea	83.0	79.9	86.0	6.1
11	Sweden	82.8	81.0	84.6	3.6
12	France	82.7	79.7	85.5	5.8
13	Malta	82.5	80.7	84.3	3.6
14	Norway	82.4	80.4	84.4	4.0
15	Canada	82.4	80.4	84.4	4.0
16	Ireland	82.3	80.7	83.9	3.3
17	Netherlands	82.3	80.6	84.0	3.4
18	New Zealand	82.3	80.6	84.0	3.5
19	Luxembourg	82.3	80.2	84.3	4.2
20	Greece	82.2	79.8	84.7	4.9
21	Portugal	82.1	79.0	84.9	5.9
22	Finland	81.9	79.1	84.7	5.7
23	Andorra	81.9			
24	Belgium	81.6	79.3	83.9	4.7
25	Austria	81.5	79.2	83.9	4.8
26	Germany	81.3	78.9	83.7	4.8
27	United Kingdom	81.3	79.6	83.0	3.5
28	Slovenia	81.3	78.6	84.0	5.5
29	Cyprus	81.0	78.9	83.0	4.2
30	Denmark	80.9	78.9	82.9	5.0
31	Liechtenstein	80.7			
32	Costa Rica	80.3	77.7	82.9	5.2
33	Chile	80.2	77.8	82.4	4.8
34	Qatar	80.2	79.1	82.0	4.8
35	Czech Republic	79.4	76.8	81.9	5.2
36	Barbados	79.2	77.8	80.5	2.7
37	United States	79.1	76.6	81.6	5.0
38	Lebanon	78.9	77.1	80.9	3.7
39	Maldives	78.9	77.5	80.8	3.7
40	Estonia	78.8	74.4	82.7	8.4
41	Cuba	78.8	76.8	80.8	3.9
42	Poland	78.7	74.8	82.6	7.8
43	Albania	78.6	77.0	80.2	7.8
44	Croatia	78.5	75.3	81.6	6.4
45	Panama	78.5	75.4	81.8	6.4
46	Dominica	78.2			
47	United Arab Emirates	78.0	77.3	79.3	2.1
48	Uruguay	77.9	74.1	81.5	7.4
143	Pakistan	67.3	66.3	68.3	1.9
144	Myanmar	67.1	64.0	70.1	6.1
145	Djibouti	67.1	65.1	69.4	4.2
146	Madagascar	67.0	65.4	68.7	3.2
147	Kenya	66.7	64.3	69.0	4.7
148	Ethiopia	66.6	64.7	68.5	3.8
149	Gabon	66.5	64.4	68.7	4.7
150	Eritrea	66.3	64.2	68.6	4.4
151	Yemen	66.1	64.4	67.8	3.4
152	Tanzania	65.5	63.6	67.2	3.6
153	Sudan	65.3	63.5	67.2	3.6
154	Mauritania	64.9	63.3	66.5	3.2
155	Afghanistan	64.8	63.4	66.4	3.0
156	Congo, Republic of	64.6	63.1	66.0	2.9
157	Papua New Guinea	64.5	63.3	65.8	2.6
158	Comoros	64.3	62.6	66.1	3.5
159	Malawi	64.3	61.1	67.4	6.2
160	South Africa	64.1	60.7	67.7	6.9
161	Ghana	64.1	63.0	65.2	2.2
162	Liberia	64.1	62.7	65.5	2.8
163	Haiti	64.0	61.8	66.2	4.3
164	Zambia	63.9	60.8	66.9	5.9
165	Namibia	63.7	60.7	66.5	5.8
166	Uganda	63.4	61.0	65.6	4.5
167	Niger	62.4	61.3	63.6	2.3
168	Gambia	62.1	60.7	63.5	2.8
169	Benin	61.8	60.2	63.3	3.1
170	Guinea	61.6	60.9	62.1	1.2
171	Burkina Faso	61.6	60.7	62.3	1.5
172	Burundi	61.6	59.8	63.4	3.6
	Sub-Saharan Africa	**61.5**	**59.8**	**63.3**	**3.1**
173	Zimbabwe	61.5	59.8	62.9	3.1
174	Angola	61.2	58.4	64.0	5.6
175	Togo	61.0	60.2	61.9	1.7
176	Mozambique	60.9	57.8	63.7	5.9
177	Congo, Democratic Republic of the	60.7	59.1	62.2	3.0
178	Eswatini	60.2	56.0	64.8	8.7
179	Cameroon	59.3	58.0	60.6	2.5
180	Mali	59.3	58.5	60.1	1.5
181	Equatorial Guinea	58.7	57.7	59.9	2.2
182	Guinea-Bissau	58.3	56.3	60.2	3.9
183	South Sudan	57.9	56.4	59.4	3.0
184	Côte d'Ivoire	57.8	56.6	59.1	2.4
185	Nigeria	54.7	53.8	55.6	1.7
186	Sierra Leone	54.7	53.9	55.5	1.6
187	Lesotho	54.3	51.2	57.6	6.4
188	Chad	54.2	52.8	55.7	2.8
189	Central African Republic	53.3	51.1	55.5	4.4

Source: UNPD United Nations Development Programme

life expectancy Lebenserwartung — **lifespan** Lebensdauer — **United Nations Development Programme** Entwicklungsprogramm der Vereinten Nationen — **column** Säule — **ranking** Rang — **tie** Gleichstand — **birth cohort** Geburtsjahrgang — **on average** im Durchschnitt — **to drop** fallen — **closely related** eng miteinander verbunden — **wealth** Reichtum; Wohlstand — **notable exception** bemerkenswerte Ausnahme — **factor** Faktor — **to influence** beeinflussen — **to lead to** führen zu — **availability** Verfügbarkeit — **affordable** bezahlbar — **health care** medizinische Versorgung — **below** unter — **to play a role** eine Rolle spielen — **to lose** verlieren

Step 2 Description and analysis of the table and data

2. **Describe the table. The keywords may help you.**

simple • five columns • ranking • name • each country • average life expectancy

accompanied by • flag

ties • several places • data • divided by males and females • missing • Andorra, Liechtenstein and

not complete • only includes • ranked 1-48 and

3. **Use the following questions to write your analysis. Write complete sentences.**

— What are the top and the last country on the list?

— What is the life expectancy of people born there in 2018?

— What is the difference in the life expectancy of the countries at the top and the bottom of the list?

— Where are most of the countries at the top of the list located?

— Where are the ones at the bottom of the list?

— How are the life expectancies of women and men different?

— What is the average difference?

— Does this average difference change between the countries at the top of the list and at the bottom?

— How is life expectancy related to the wealth of the country you are born in?

— Do you see any exceptions to this rule on the list?

Step 3 Evaluation: Your opinion

Write an evaluation of the data. These questions may help you.

— What information might help you understand differences in life expectancy in various countries?

— Did anything on the list surprise you? Can you think of possible explanations?

— What other statistics about life expectancies would interest you?

....

....

....

....

....

....

....

....

TABLE 3

Generation Alpha

Culture / Technology

Your turn

TIP This table doesn't include the numerical data typical of most tables. You may, therefore, find it helpful to combine your analysis and evaluation.

origin Herkunft — **slang term** umgangssprachliches/r Wort/Ausdruck — **social marker** h.: wichtiges gesellschaftliches Ereignis — **iconic** kultig; ikonisch — **leadership style** Führungsstil — **screen content** Bildschirminhalt — **economy** Wirtschaft — **(Great) Depression** (Große) Depression; Weltwirtschaftskrise — **WW2 = World War Two** der Zweite Weltkrieg — **if you please** wenn ich bitten darf — **baby boomer** jd., der den geburtenstarken Jahrgängen der Nachkriegszeit angehört — **groovy** cool — **way out** super — **to direct** leiten — **ironically** ironischerweise — **to be named after s.th.** nach etw. benannt werden — **label** Etikett — **moniker** h.: Bezeichnung; Hinweis — **to span** umfassen — **dude** Kumpel — **ace** genial — **rad(ical)** radikal; krass — **as if** Von wegen! — **wicked** geil — **stock market** Börse — **crash** Absturz — **to coordinate** koordinieren; abstimmen — **to follow** nachkommen — **bling** Klunker — **funky** flippig — **Doh!** wird verwendet, wenn man gerade etw. Dummes gemacht hat — **foshizz = for sure** echt — **whassup? = What's up?** — **era** Ära — **lit** toll — **fam = family** jd., der wie Familie ist — **bae = baby** Schatz — **to slay** die Konkurrenz schlagen — **yass (= yes) queen** Jaaaa! — **GFC = Global Financial Crisis** — **to empower** befähigen; stärken — **to coin** prägen — **to define** definieren — **extra** übertrieben — **to flex; flex** angeben; Angeberei — **to yeet** wegschmeißen — **GOAT = greatest of all time** — **to inspire** begeistern — **characteristic** Eigenschaft — **to allow** ermöglichen — **comparison** Vergleich — **to visualise** veranschaulichen — **qualitative** qualitativ — **valuable** wertvoll — **technologically advanced** technisch fortgeschritten — **native speaker** Muttersprachler(in) — **matter of opinion** Ansichtssache — **to be associated with s.th.** mit etw. in Zusammenhang stehen

Describe and analyse the table. Use a separate sheet of paper.

CATEGORY	BUILDERS	BABY BOOMERS	GENERATION X	GENERATION Y	GENERATION Z	GENERATION α
Name origin	The generation that built the economy, infrastructure and society after the Depression and WW2.	The post-war baby boom that created an economic boom.	Ironically named after Douglas Coupland's anti-label moniker - "just call us X". Note: spans 15 years.	The letter that followed X, also known as Millennials.	Following from Y, the end of an era and the end of a millennium.	Coined by McCrindle to define the start of a whole new era. Follows scientific naming (Greek alphabet).
Slang terms	We prefer proper English if you please Born: < 1946 Age: 75+	Be cool, Peace, Groovy, Way out Born: 1946-1964 Age: 56-74	Dude, Ace, Rad, As if, Wicked Born: 1965-1979 Age: 41-55	Bling, Funky, Doh, Foshizz, Whassup? Born: 1980-1994 Age: 26-40	lit, fam, bae, slay, yass queen Born: 1995-2009 Age: 11-25	extra, flex, yeet, insta, GOAT Born: 2010-2024 Age: under 11
Social markers	World War II 1939-1945	Moon landing 1969	Stock market crash 1987	September 11 2001	GFC 2008	Trump/Brexit 2016 COVID-19 2020
Iconic cars	Model T Ford Final, 1927	Ford Mustang 1964	Holden Commodore 1978	Toyota Prius 1997	Tesla Model S 2012	Autonomous vehicles 2020s
Iconic toys	Roller skates	Frisbee	Rubik's cube	BMX bike	Folding scooter	Fidget spinner
Music devices	Record player LP, 1948	Audio cassette 1962	Walkman 1979	iPod 2001	Spotify 2008	Smart speakers Now
Leadership styles	Controlling	Directing	Coordinating	Guiding	Empowering	Inspiring
Screen content	Cinema	TV	VCR	Internet	Device	Streaming

For more on the generations: **mccrindle.com**
For a detailed report: **generationalpha.com**
To book a speaker for your next event: **mccrindlespeakers.com**
mccrindle

VENN DIAGRAMS

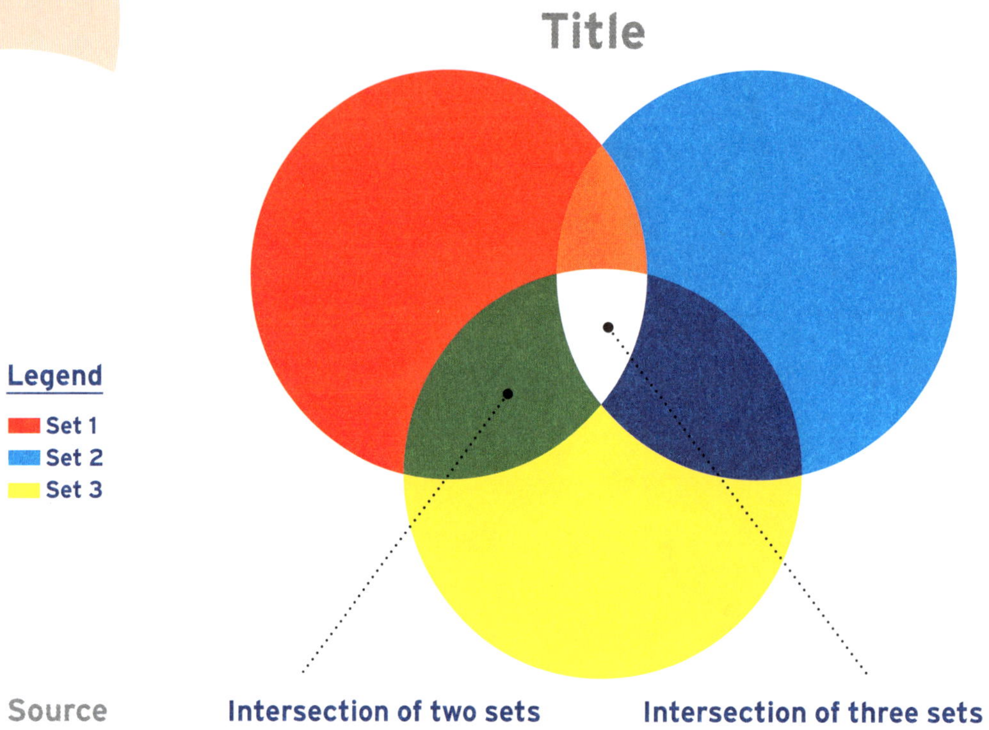

FACT FILE

Venn diagrams show two or more sets (groups of things) in shapes (usually circles) that overlap. In the intersections (overlapping areas) are things the groups have in common. Venn diagrams often don't include any numbers.

- Venn diagrams are named after British mathematician *John Venn*, who wrote about them in 1880. However, he didn't give them the name **Venn diagram**. That was done by mathematician *CI Lewis* who named them in 1918.
- These diagrams can be very complex and include seven oder more sets.
- Venn diagrams can show empty sections.

intersection Überlappungsbereich; Schnittmenge — **set** Menge — **to overlap** überlappen; s. überschneiden; **overlapping areas** — **subset** Untermenge — **actual** tatsächlich — **to be named after s.o.** nach jdm. benannt werden — **mathematician** Mathematiker(in)

GUIDELINES FOR DESCRIBING AND ANALYSING A VENN DIAGRAM

- How does the Venn diagram **look**? What **information** does it contain? How is this information **shown** in the diagram?
  It's made of two / three / … (sets in overlapping) circles / ovals / …
  The (set in the) blue / red / … circle shows / represents / contains …
  The circle at the top / on the right / … is labelled …
- What is the most **meaningful** information? This may be where the shapes overlap, but it can also be important to see which information does not overlap.
  The diagram shows that …, …, and … all have … in common.
  The diagram shows that (only) … and … do not have … in common.

VENN DIAGRAM 1

Guided

Avoid the Three Cs

The coronavirus pandemic

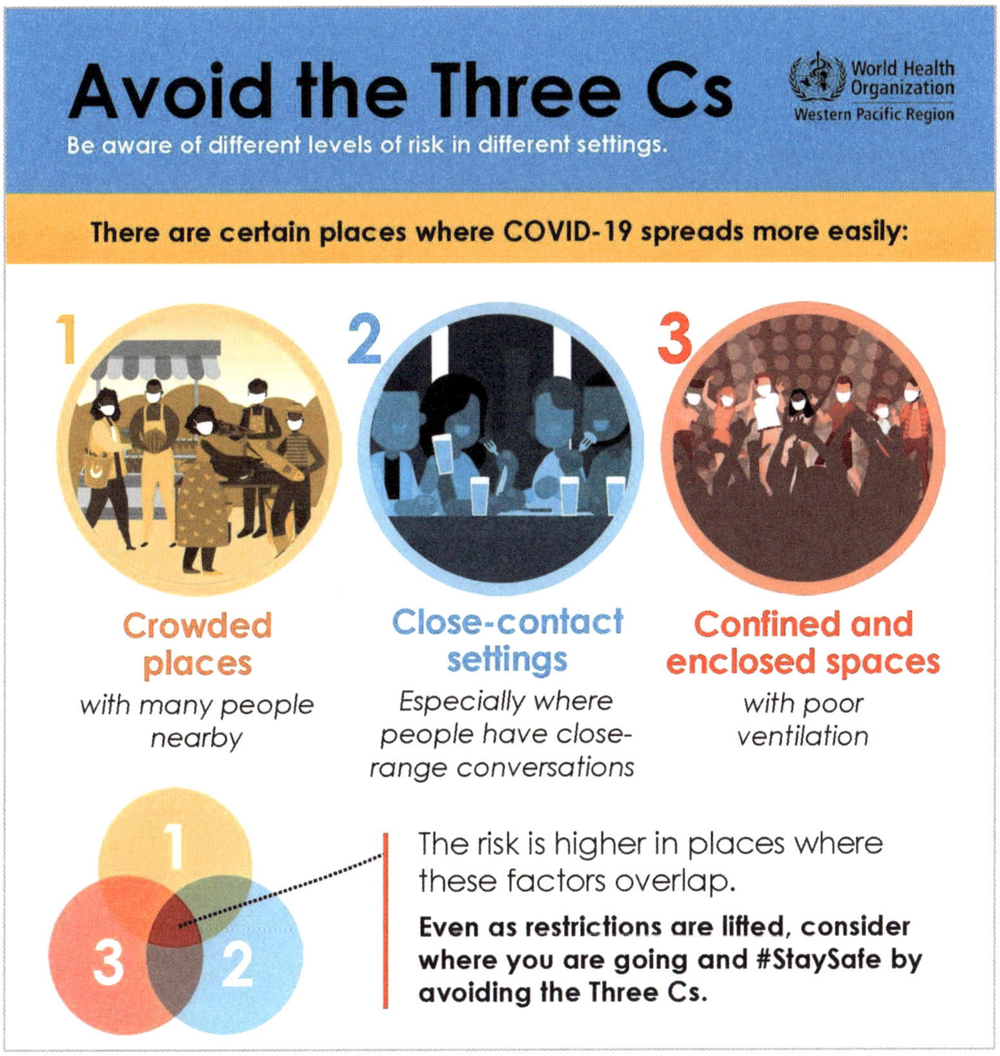

to be aware of s.th. s. etw. bewusst sein — **level** Niveau — **risk** Risiko — **setting** Umgebung — **to spread** s. verbreiten — **close-range** aus kurzer Entfernung — **confined** beengt — **enclosed** umschlossen — **poor** schlecht — **ventilation** Belüftung — **to lift a restriction** ein Verbot aufheben — **to correspond** entsprechen — **to represent** darstellen — **arrow** Pfeil — **step** Schritt

Step 1 Basic information

1. **Fill in the missing information. You do not need to write complete sentences. The sample Venn diagram and information on page 44 can help you.**

a) What is the **title** of the Venn diagram? ....

....

....

b) What is the **source** of the Venn diagram? ....

....

....

c) How does the Venn diagram **look**? ....

....

....

d) What **information** does the Venn diagram contain? ....

....

....

e) How is this information **shown** in the Venn diagram? ....

....

....

....

....

Step 2 Description and analysis of the data

2. **Circle the correct words.**

The Venn diagram (1) looks / shows / asks how your risk of getting COVID-19
(2) decreases / remains / grows with each of the three risk factors.
The (3) intersections / crossings / sets of two factors are darker than
(4) single / only / triple factors. The intersection of all three factors is even darker.
A(n) (5) arrow / line / lead next to the diagram (6) aims / presents / points to the intersection
of the (7) three / two / whole factors and says that the 'risk is higher in places where these factors overlap.
This means that darker colours are more (8) interesting / meaningful / overlapping than lighter colours.

Step 3 Evaluation: Your opinion

Write an evaluation of the Venn diagram. These questions may help you.

— Do you think that the Venn diagram presents the information in a helpful way?

— Do you think that the way it presents the information could be improved?

VENN DIAGRAM 2*

Semi-guided

British Isles

British Isles / Geography / Politics

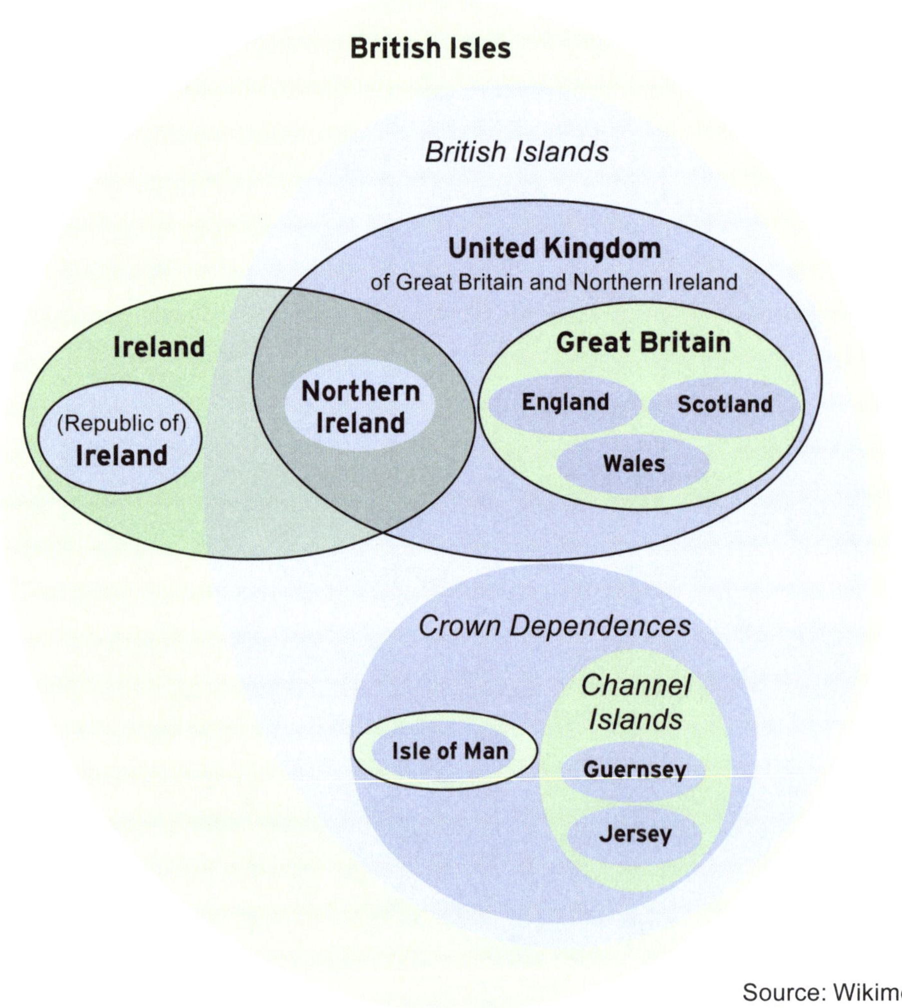

Source: Wikimedia Commons

Geographical features

- Island
- Archipelago

Legal distinctions

- Sovereign State
- Other legal entity or description

FACT FILE

* This is technically an Euler diagram.

— Euler diagrams only show actual relationships, so there will be no blank areas that might be in a Venn diagram.

— Euler diagrams can include subsets, meaning that one set may be completely within another.

— Euler diagrams were created by Swiss mathematician Leonhard Euler in the 1700s.

geographical feature landschaftliche Gegebenheit – **archipelago** Inselgruppe – **legal distinction** juristischer Unterschied – **sovereign state** souveräner Staat – **entity** Rechtskörper – **crown dependency** Kronbesitz

Step 1 Basic information

1. **Write a short introduction that gives the title and the source of the diagram.**

....

....

2. **Describe the diagram.**

....

....

....

....

Step 2 Description and analysis of the data

3. **Answer the questions in complete sentences.**

a) What is the largest set in this diagram?

....

b) How many subsets are there? What are they?

....

....

....

c) How many islands does the diagram show? What are they?

....

....

d) What does Northern Ireland belong to geographically?

....

e) What does Northern Ireland belong to politically?

....

f) What belongs to Great Britain?

g) What are the crown dependencies of the British Isles?

Step 3 Evaluation: Your opinion

Write an evaluation of the diagram. These questions may help you.

— How well do you think the diagram shows the relationships of the British Isles?

— What would you change?

VENN DIAGRAM 3

Your turn

Trump's Unique Feat

US / Politics

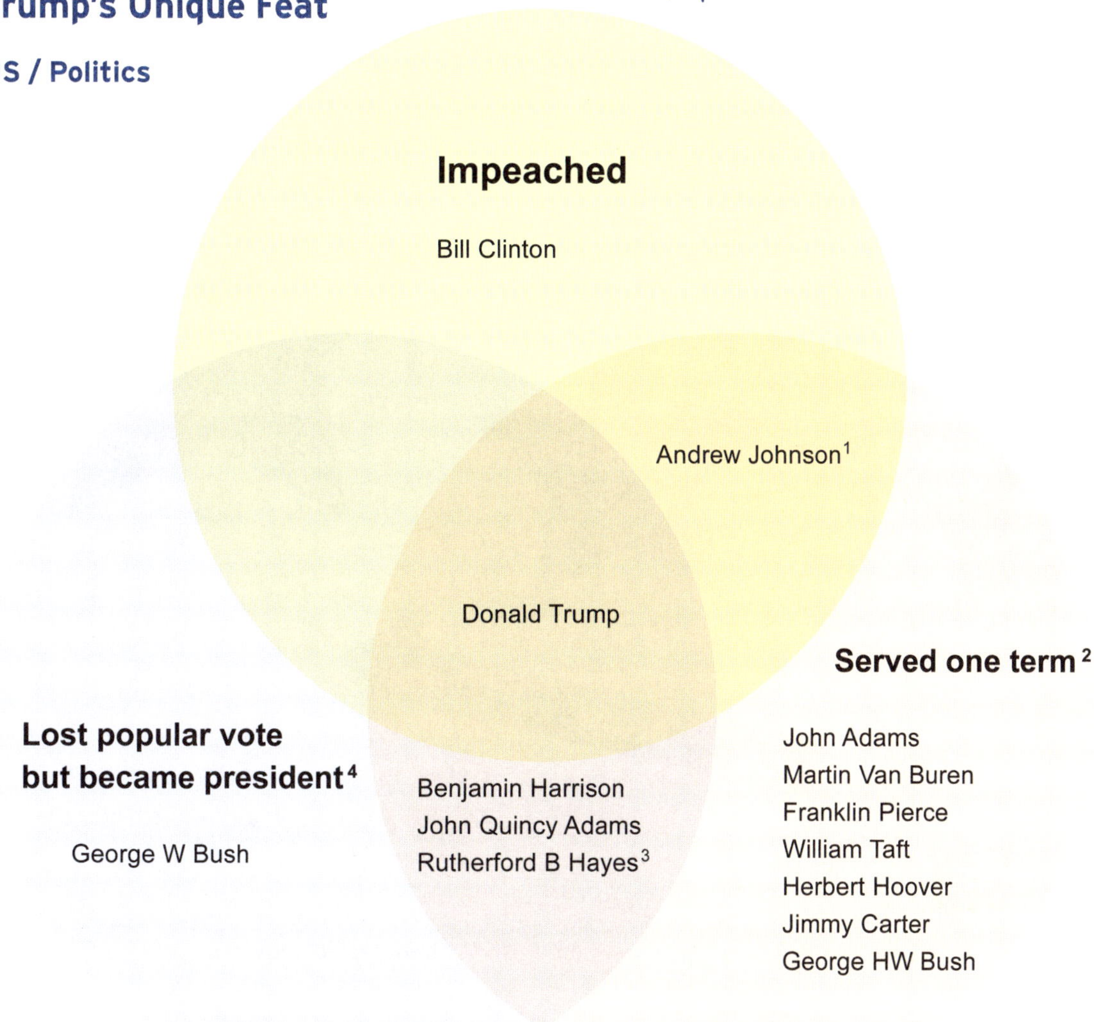

Background INFO

1. *Andrew Johnson* was not elected and served slightly less than a full term. He became president after *Abraham Lincoln* was assassinated. He is included in the diagram because he is one of the few presidents who was impeached.
2. This list does not include presidents who died in office, did not run for a second term, or were not elected but became president after the death or resignation of the previous president.
3. *Rutherford B Hayes* did not run for re-election. He is included in the diagram as one of the few presidents who lost the popular vote.
4. This can happen because of the Electoral College. A candidate can lose the popular vote but still become president by gaining the majority of the Electoral College votes.

Describe and analyse the Venn diagram. Use a separate sheet of paper.

unique einzigartig — **feat** Leistung — **to impeach** wegen Amtsvergehen verklagen — **term** Amtszeit — **to serve** h.: (eine Amtszeit) durchlaufen — **popular vote** h.: absolute Mehrheit der Volksabstimmung — **slightly** etwas — **to assassinate** ein Attentat verüben — **to run** h.: kandidieren — **resignation** Rücktritt

INFOGRAPHICS

Infographics may contain numbers in

percentages: 25% = twenty-five percent

fractions: ¼ = one quarter = one in four

ratios: 3:1 = three to one

currency: $1,000 = one thousand dollars; £500 = 500 pounds

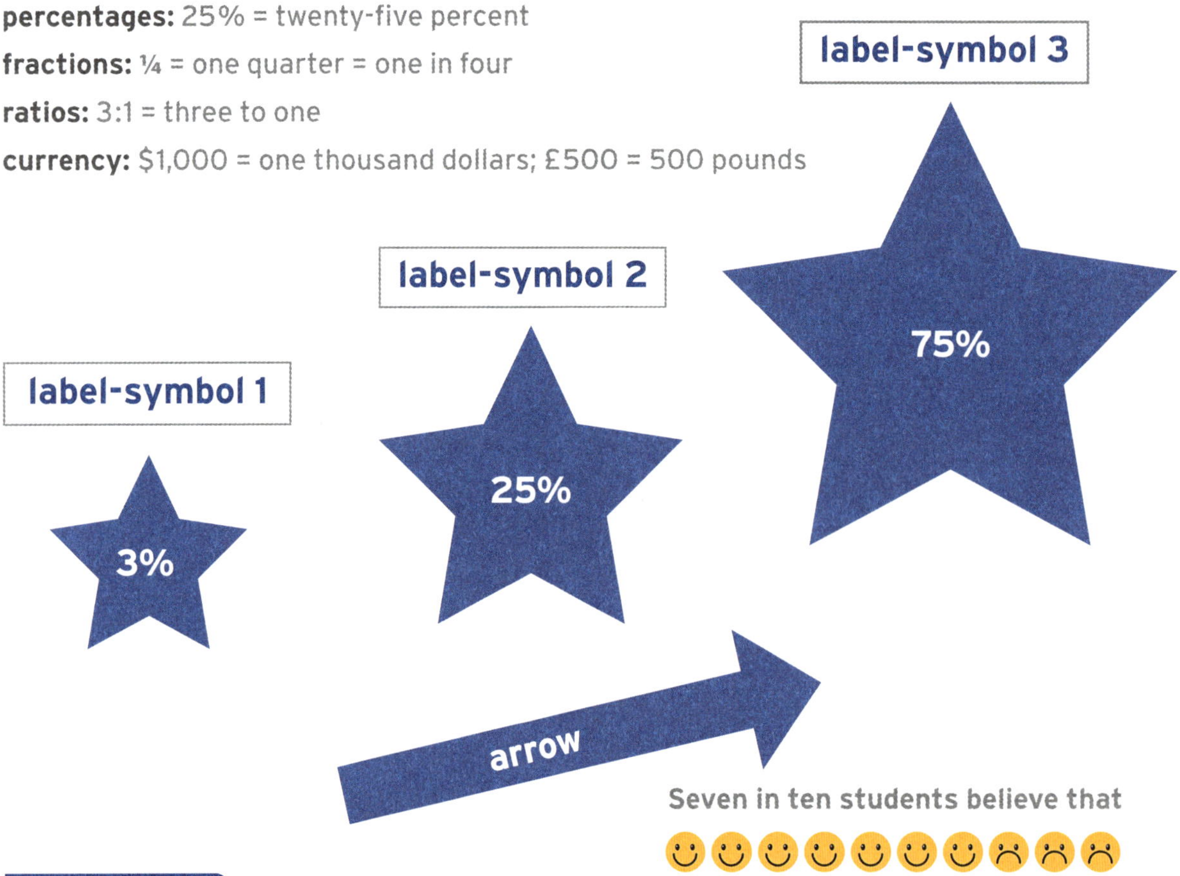

FACT FILE

An infographic uses symbols or pictures and a small amount of text to present an overview of a topic in a way that is fast and easy to understand. A large infographic may include pie charts, bar charts, or other types of visuals.

— Infographics are often made to be eye-catching and entertaining.

— Some are small and simple. Some are large and complex.

— You will find infographics in school-books, newspapers, and magazines and in many other places.

overview Überblick — **eye-catching** auffallend; ins Auge springend — **to break down** aufgliedern; vereinfachen; analysieren

GUIDELINES FOR DESCRIBING AND ANALYSING AN INFOGRAPHIC

— What symbols or pictures are used to present the information?
There is / are … / The background is / symbols are (green) … /

— What kinds of visuals are used (statistics, pie charts, tables, etc.)?
The infographic contains a pie chart / a bar chart / symbols …

— What information is included in the infographic?
The infographic includes the names / dates / number … of …

INFOGRAPHIC 1

Guided

Top 5 Languages Spoken in Australia

Australia / Multiculturalism

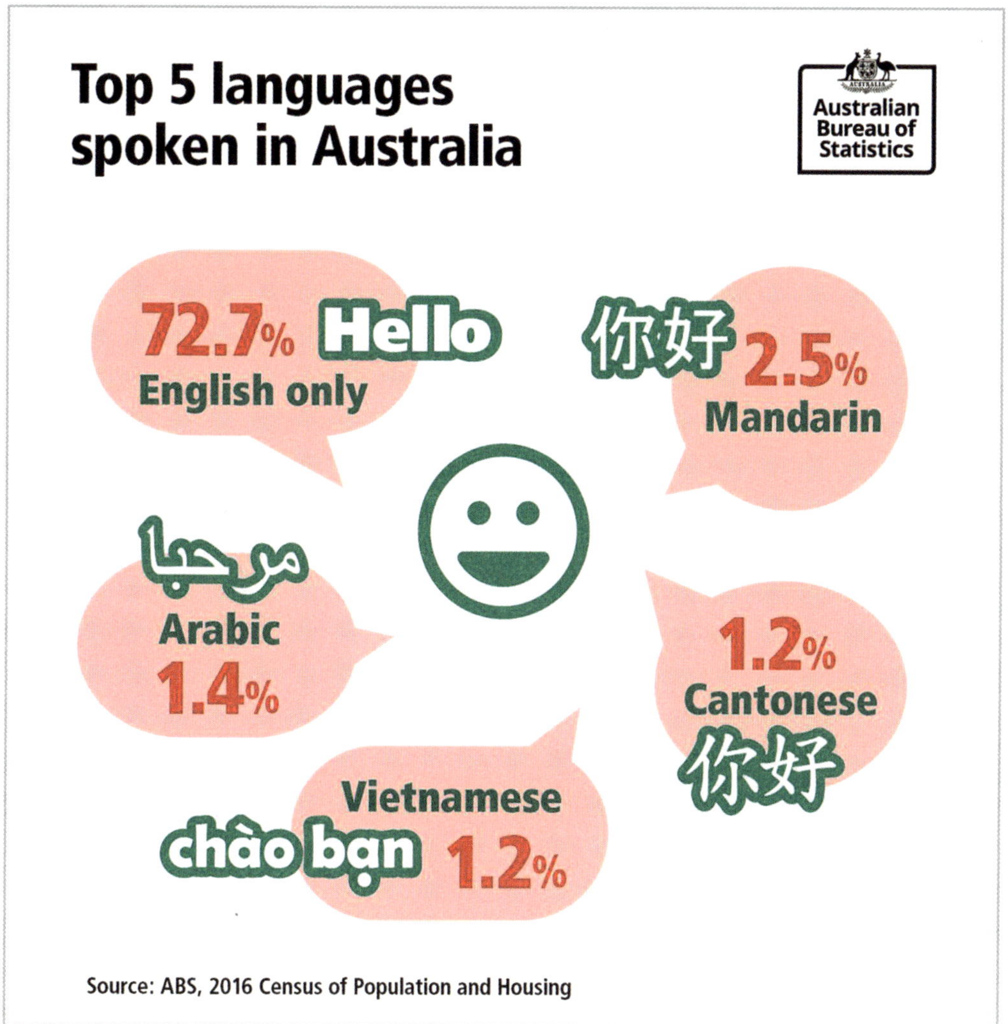

bureau Amt — **census** Volkszählung — **population** Bevölkerung — **housing** Wohnraum — **to state** sagen; angeben — **smiley face** lächelndes Gesicht; Smiley — **speech bubble** Sprechblase — **to add up to** zusammen ergeben — **great majority** große Mehrheit

Step 1 Basic information

1. Fill in the missing information. You do not need to write complete sentences. The sample infographic and information on page 52 can help you.

a) What is the **title** of the infographic?

....

b) What is the **source** of the information in the infographic?

....

....

c) What **symbols** are used to present the information?

....

d) What **information** is included in the infographic?

....

....

....

....

Step 2 Description and analysis of the infograhic and data

2. Complete the text with the correct languages and numbers.

The five languages in the speech bubbles are .... only, ...,
...................................., ..., and ....

The largest is ...., which is the only language spoken by most of the population. The next largest is ...., followed by .... and .... and ....

The great majority (............%) of Australians only speak .... The other four languages only add up to a total of ....%. That means that about a fifth of Australians either speak another language, speak more than .... language, or didn't state a language.

When you add together the people who speak Mandarin (............%) and Cantonese (............%), you can see that ....% speak a Chinese language. This means that there are probably a lot of people in Australia whose families originally came from China.

Step 3 Evaluation: Your opinion

Write an evaluation of the data. These questions may help you.

— Did anything in the data surprise you?

— Is there any additional information you would like to have?

— What do or don't you like about the way the data is presented?

INFOGRAPHIC 2

Semi-guided

St Patrick's Day by the Numbers

US / Ireland / Culture / Holidays / Immigration

by the numbers in Zahlen ausgedrückt — **dye** Farbstoff; **to dye** färben — **to turn s.th.** ... etw. ... machen / werden lassen — **40 lbs (pounds)** ≈ 20,41 kg — **length of time** Zeitspanne — **shamrock** Kleeblatt — **to illustrate** veranschaulichen; verbildlichen — **symbol** Symbol; **to symbolise** symbolisieren — **to highlight** hervorheben — **peace sign** Friedenszeichen — **area** Fläche

Step 1 Basic information

1. **Write a short introduction that gives the title and source of the infographic.**

2. Number the parts of the sentence in the correct order. The punctuation and capitalisation will help you. One part has already been numbered for you. Write the sentence.

behind	contains information	is illustrated by	in the US
	2		
about the numbers	St Patrick's Day	three large symbols	The infographic

....

....

Step 2 Description and analysis of the infographic and data

3. Collect words and phrases to describe the appearance of each element in the infographic: the symbol, colours used, etc. Some words have already been written for you.

The background	The first symbol 	The second symbol 	The third symbol 
shamrocks	yellow		

4. Use the words from task 3 to write a description of the infographic.

....

....

....

....

....

....

....

5. **Describe the meaning of each element. Why is it used? One element has already been described.**

The background	The first symbol 	The second symbol 	The third symbol 
	symbolises dyeing the river		

6. **What kind of information is presented with the symbols?**
Match each symbol with one kind of information. There are six words you don't need.

a) The first symbol
b) The second symbol
c) The third symbol

1 height
2 temperature
3 a length of time
4 price
5 year
6 volume
7 amount
8 area
9 speed

7. **Use the information from tasks 5 and 6 to write an analysis of the infographic.**

....

....

....

....

....

....

....

Step 3 Evaluation: Your opinion

Write an evaluation of the data. These questions may help you.

— Do you think that the colours and symbols were a good choice for the infographic? Why or why not?

— What do these facts tell you about American culture and Chicago?

INFOGRAPHIC 3

Your turn

Dirty Beaches: 24 Hours of Trash

Environment

worldwide weltweit — **cleanup event** Putzaktion — **cigarette butt** Zigarettenkippe — **food wrapper** Lebensmittelverpackung — **straw** Trinkhalm — **stirrer** Rührstäbchen — **container** Behälter — **lid** Deckel — **foam** Schaumstoff — **coastal** Küsten- — **community** Gemeinde — **to rally together** s. versammeln — **conservancy** Naturschutz

Describe and analyse the infographic. Use a separate sheet of paper.

ANSWER KEY!

BAR CHART 1

America's Favourite Fourth of July Foods

Step 1

1. **a)** America's Favourite Fourth of July Foods: Food Sales in the Two Weeks around Independence Day
   b) Nielsen
   c) Simple (bar chart)
   d) foods (each with a small picture)
   e) dollars
   f) food sales in millions of dollars for the two weeks ending 9 July 2016

2. **a)** The **title** of this bar chart is 'America's Favourite Fourth of July Foods: Food Sales in the Two Weeks around Independence Day'.
   b) The **source** of the information in the bar chart is Nielsen.
   c) It is a simple type of **bar chart.**
   d) The vertical **axis** shows ten different foods, each with a small picture.
   e) The **horizontal** axis shows millions of dollars.
   f) Each **bar** shows food sales in millions of dollars for the two weeks ending 9 July 2016.

Step 2

3. The data shows that beef had the highest ($803.9 m) amount in sales. It sold more than twice as much as chicken, which is the next food on the list. Americans paid less ($114.7 m) for tomatoes than any other food on the list. Of the ten foods, seven are types of meat.
4. Americans spend more money on meat than on fruits and vegetables.
5. Americans obviously eat a lot of meat on the Fourth of July. However, meat is usually more expensive than fruits and vegetables. It is possible that Americans just spend more money on expensive meat than on inexpensive fruits and vegetables.

Step 3

Sample answer

I didn't expect that Americans would still eat so much meat. I thought that a lot of Americans are eating more healthily these days. I'd like to know how much of each kind of food they eat (for example, in weight) and not just how much they pay for each food.

BAR CHART 2

The UK's Housework Gender Roles

Step 1

1. The title of these two bar charts is 'The UK's Housework Gender Roles: Housework Tasks Most Often Solely Done by Men or by Women in UK Households'. They are simple bar charts. The source is YouGov, which surveyed 1,314 UK adults currently living with a partner on 14–15 November 2019.
2. The vertical axis of each chart shows five different housework tasks. The horizontal axis shows men/women in percentages.
3. 5 are orange.
   7 the percentage of women/men
   4 the bars for men
   2 are yellow
   6 Each bar shows
   3 and
   8 who do that task solely.
   1 The bars for women

Step 2

4. 1 greater
   2 between
   3 percentage
   4 just
   5 While
   6 house
   7 gardening

Step 3

Sample answer

I was surprised that women do so much more housework than men. I thought that there would be more gender equality by 2019.

BAR CHART 3

7 in 10 American Teens Use TikTok

The title of this bar chart is '7 in 10 American Teens Use TikTok: % of US Teens Who Use the Following Social Media Platforms at Least Once a Month'. It is a simple bar chart. The source of the data is Piper Sandler. It is based on a survey of 9,800 US teens conducted 2020.

The vertical axis shows seven different social media platforms. The horizontal axis shows the US teen population in percentages. The bar for each social media platform has a different colour.

The data shows that Instagram was the most popular platform: 84% of teens used it at least once a month. Next is Snapchat with 80%. LinkedIn was the least popular platforms. Only 3% of teens used it at least once a month.

Almost all teens used a social media platform at least once a month. The numbers add up to a lot more than 100%. This shows that most teens use more than one social media platform.

A month is a long time. I think most teens use social media platforms almost every day. It's too bad that the bar chart doesn't show daily or weekly use. It would be interesting to compare the most popular social media platforms used by teens in the US and in Germany.

LINE CHART 1

US Cases Drop as Europe Faces Third Wave

Step 1

1. a) US Cases Drop as Europe Faces Third Wave: Seven-Day Rolling Average of Newly Confirmed COVID-19 Cases in the US and the European Union'

   b) Johns Hopkins University

   c) the number of newly confirmed COVID-19 cases on a scale of 0 to 300,000

   d) a timeline from March 2020 to 14 March 2021

   e) the seven-day rolling average number of newly confirmed cases in the United States

   f) the seven-day rolling average number of newly confirmed cases in the European Union

Step 2

2. The data shows that both the US and the EU started off with about zero cases in March 2020. The number of cases rose a little more quickly in the EU than in the US. Both the US and EU reached about 30,000 cases at the end of March. In the EU, the number of cases began to fall at the beginning of April.

   By the middle of May 2020, the number of new cases dropped to only a few thousand per week in the EU. The number of cases in the US stayed at about 20,000–25,000 until the middle of June, when it began to rise steeply again. Numbers in the EU stayed fairly low, but they began to rise sharply in late summer and early autumn. The number of cases in the EU passed the number in the US at the beginning of October. After early November, the general trend was downwards in the EU but upwards in the US. In January 2021, the number of cases was around 250,000 in the US and 150,000 in the EU. By March 2021, the EU had more than twice as many COVID cases as the US.

Step 3

I was surprised that the US sometimes had lower numbers of new COVID-19 cases than the EU. A good example is in October and November 2020. I thought that the US always had more new cases than the EU after the beginning of the pandemic.

I think that the trends in the number of cases were due to lockdowns, rules about masks, and the results of the US 2020 presidential election. It would be interesting to compare the dates of the lockdowns, introduction of mask rules, and the presidential election with the trends on the chart.

LINE CHART 2

The Steady Rise of Podcasts

Step 1

1. The title of this line chart is 'The Steady Rise of Podcasts: Percentage and Number of Americans (12+) Who Have Listened to a Podcast in the Past'. The sources of the data are Edison Research and Triton Digital.

   The vertical axis shows the percentage of Americans who have listened to a podcast in the past on a scale of 0% to 60%. The horizontal axis is a timeline of the years 2006 to 2020.

   The dark blue line shows the percentage of Americans who have listened to a podcast. The light blue line shows the percentage of Americans who have listened to a podcast in the past month.

Step 2

2. The number of Americans who have listened to a podcast is rising.
3. The percentage of Americans who had ever listened to a podcast rose from about 10% in 2006 to about 55% (around 155 million people) in 2020. The percentage of Americans who had listened to a podcast in the past month rose from about 10% in 2006 to about 37% (around 104 million people) in 2020.
4. As the title of the line chart says, the data shows a steady rise of podcasts. However, there was a small dip in 2013. The information in the footnote for that year explains this dip. It says that 'the source changed the definition of what qualifies as a podcast'. It seems that the change meant that fewer programmes qualified as podcasts: that led to a dip in the numbers.

Step 3

I thought it's interesting that about half of all Americans have listened to a podcast. I'd like to know the ages of the people who listen. For example, it would be nice to know if more younger or older people listen to podcasts. I think that podcasts are becoming more popular and that these numbers are still rising.

LINE CHART 3

Number of Kids per Household on Decline

The title of this line chart is 'Number of Kids per Household on Decline'.

The source of the information is the (Australian) Census of Population and Housing, 2016.

The vertical axis shows Australian households in percentage on a scale of 5% to 21%. The horizontal axis shows the years 1966 and 2016.

There are three lines on the chart. The blue line shows the percentage of households with one child. The green line shows the percentage of households with two children. The red line shows the percentage of households with three or more children. Each line has only two data points: 1966 and 2016.

The data shows that the percentage of households with children in each category fell from 1966 to 2016. The greatest decline was in the category of households with three or more children. This was the largest category in 1966 but the smallest category in 2016. From 1966 to 2016, it fell from 20% to 6%.

I knew that people don't have as many children today as in the past, but I was still surprised that so few households have three or more children. It would be interesting to see the average number of children per household in different countries, including Australia and Germany.

PIE CHART 1

Fewer Americans Are Driving to Work

Step 1

1. a) The title of these pie charts is 'Fewer Americans Are Driving to Work: Share of US Workers Aged 18+ Who Commute to Work Using the Following Means'.

   b) Gallup

   c) 1,024 people

   d) August 2007

   e) August 2018

   f) Each pie chart is divided into seven coloured segments.

   g) a different type of transportation

   h) the description and size of each segment/ a description of each means of transportation and the percentage of people who use it

Step 2

2. a) drive yourself

   b) 85

   c) bicycle

   d) 0

   e) drive yourself

   f) 77

   g) bicycle

   h) 1

3. Although the percentage fell from 2007, most American workers still commuted by car in 2018.

Step 3

Although I know that Americans drive a lot, I was surprised by the percentage of Americans who get to work by car. I think a lot more Germans use other means of transportation, especially mass transportation and bikes. Since the 2020 corona pandemic, more people probably telecommute.

It would also be interesting to see how these numbers change at different times of the year. The surveys were taken in August: I think that even more people drive to work during the cold and wet winter months.

PIE CHART 2

Do Brits Miss Going to the Pub?

Step 1

1. The title of this pie chart is 'Do Brits Miss Going to the Pub?: "How Much, If at All, Do You Miss Going to the Pub?"' The source of the information is YouGov, which surveyed 2,241 British adults /adults in Great Britain on 30 June 2020. The pie chart has five segments.

2. 2 shows
   5 and the percentage of Britons
   1 Each segment
   4 the question in the title
   6 who gave that answer.
   3 a different answer to

Step 2

3. a) The coronavirus pandemic was happening in June 2020.

   b) People didn't go to the pubs because they were closed. People were also worried about the virus.

   c) The largest segment of the pie chart is 'Not very much' (28%). The smallest is 'Very much' (7%).

   d) Although many people see pubs as an important part of British life, only about one quarter (27%) of the people missed going to them a fair bit or very much. Almost a quarter of the people said that they don't go to the pub at all.

Step 3

I expected that more Brits would miss going to the pub at least a fair bit. I think that people missed the pub more later in the pandemic. Maybe people also missed going to the pub less in spring and summer because they could do more activities outside.

PIE CHART 3

Women Are an Endangered Species in Hollywood

The title of these three pie charts is 'Women Are an Endangered Species in Hollywood: Females Behind the Camera in 2014'. The source of the information is 'Inequality in 700 Popular Films: Examining Portrayals of Character Gender, Race & LGBT Status from 2007 to 2014'.

The captions of the three pie charts are Directors, Writers, and Producers. Each pie chart only has one segment. Those segments show the percentage of women in that position in Hollywood.

The pie charts show that women directed only 1.9% of Hollywood films. Women wrote 11.2% of the films and produced 18.9%.

The percentage of women behind the camera is very small in all three professions, but it's interesting to see that the percentage of women producers and writers is much greater than the percentage of directors. Are fewer women interested in being directors than writers and producers? Or don't they get these jobs? I asked myself the same questions about all three professions. Are fewer women interested in these jobs? Or is it because of gender discrimination?

MAP 1

Hardest Hit by Extreme Weather Conditions

Step 1

a) Hardest Hit by Extreme Weather Conditions

b) Germanwatch

c) the world

d) 1999–2018

Step 2

A4 • B5 • C2 • D6 • E3

Step 3

This map shows a period of 19 years. It doesn't show how countries have been moving up and down in the rankings in that time period. We don't know what the situation was like in certain years. We only see the whole period.
It would also be interesting to know the reasons for each country's ranking. Germany is orange, but we don't know what kind of weather caused this ranking.
It's interesting that a tiny place like Puerto Rico* is just as important in the rankings as a huge country like Russia or Canada. If the data were shown by geographic region and not by country, the rankings might look a lot different.
*Puerto Rico is a US territory and a commonwealth. It has its own local government but is not an independent country. The US president is its head of state.

MAP 2

The US Has the Highest Share of Single Parenting

Step 1

1. The title of this map is 'The US Has the Highest Share of Single Parenting: Percent of Children Younger than 18 Living in Single-Parent Households (2018)'.
   The source of the information is Pew Research Center. This map of the world uses five different colours to show this information.

Step 2

The colour of each country in the map corresponds to the percentage of its children living in single-parent households. The meaning of each colour is given in the legend. The countries with more than 15% of children in this situation are orange. The exact percentages of several of them are written on the map. The next group (6.9%–14.9%) is yellow and so on. For a few countries, there is no data available. These countries are grey.

As the title of the map says, the US has the highest percentage of single-parent households (23%). The UK is close behind with 21%. Germany is in the yellow group. Large parts of Africa, the Middle East, and Asia are light and dark blue. They are the lowest groups for which there is information. Most of the Americas and Europe are yellow and orange. They are the two highest groups. The countries without any data available are mostly in South America, Africa, and the Middle East. Australia and some Pacific island nations also belong to this group.

Many of the countries that show a low share of single parenting on the map are places where religion plays a large role: divorce and having children without being married may be less common in these countries. Several generations may be more likely to live together.

Step 3

I think what the map shows is different from what the heading says. The definition of a single-parent household used here is 'No other adults present in household except adult children'. This means that children with only one parent in the home aren't included if there is another adult living there. Children living with grandparents, aunts, uncles, or other adult relatives are not included. Children are not included if their single parent lives with any other adult. So, the real number of children living in a home with only one parent present is probably much larger. The statistics on the map only show how many children live with only one adult who isn't a sibling. The map is not good for seeing how many children actually have parents without partners.

I was surprised to see that there is no data available for Australia. Many of the other places with no data available are developing countries, but Australia isn't a developing country. I would be interested in knowing why Australia is not included. I would like to know what the numbers are like there.

MAP 3

The Countries Banning Plastic Bags

The title of this map is 'The Countries Banning Plastic Bags: National-Level Regulation to Ban / Limit the Use of Plastic Bags (2020)'. This map of the world shows which countries had or were considering a national ban on plastic bags in 2020.

The source of the information is the United Nations and media reports. The map was created by Statista.

Countries with a full or partial ban are shown in blue. Countries with a charge or tax on plastic bags are purple. Countries where a ban was or is under consideration are yellow.

The map shows that the strictest bans are mostly in Africa, Asia, and parts of South America. Europe generally has charges or taxes on bags but not bans. Only a few countries had bans under consideration in 2020. These countries were in Eastern Europe and Asia. There are no bans or charges or taxes at all in several large countries, for example, the US, Canada, Australia, and Russia.

I was very surprised that so many large countries don't have a ban on plastic bags. It looks to me that many poorer countries have stricter bans. Could this be because their people don't have the money to pay a charge or tax?

This map only shows national-level regulation. It would be interesting to know if some countries that are grey on this map have local bans.

TABLE 1

Number of Children and Poverty in American Families

Step 1

1. **a)** Number of Children and Poverty in American Families.

   b) US Census Bureau

   c) a complex table with many headings and subheadings

   d) 9

   e) 10

Step 2

1. The table is in two parts: one for males and one for females. Each half of the table has rows for three age groups: 16–24 years, 25–34 years, and 35 years and above. Within each one, we see the total population in that group and their income levels. We also see the number and percentage of people in that group living below the poverty line. The columns show the populations in groups by the number and age of children in the family.

   The data shows relationships between sex, number of children, age, and income level. Being a young parent of two or more young (under six years) children has a stronger correlation to poverty than any other factor: 28% of men and almost 40% of women in this group are poor. Least likely to live in poverty are men and women 25 to 34 years old with no children under 18 years: only around 4% of this group are poor.

3. Parents are more likely to live below the poverty line than people without children.

   Younger people are more likely to live below the poverty line than older people.

   Women are poorer than men.

   More children means less money.

Step 3

This table is so complex that I first had trouble understanding it. I really had to look hard at the data before I could see patterns.
I was shocked at how many Americans live in poverty. You can see that millions of Americans live below the poverty level. These numbers just include people aged 16 and older living in families, but parents living in poverty means kids living in poverty. It would be interesting to compare this information with poverty numbers in Germany.

TABLE 2

Countries and Regions by Life Expectancy at Birth in 2019

Step 1

The title of this table is 'Countries and Regions by Life Expectancy at Birth in 2019'. It shows the expected lifespan for people born in 2019 in different countries. The source of the table is the United Nations Development Programme.

Step 2

1. This is a very simple table with six columns, which show the ranking and name of each country in the list and the average life expectancy there. The name of each country is accompanied by its flag. There are ties for several places on the list, and data divided by males and females is missing for Andorra, Liechtenstein and Dominica.

   The table is not complete because it only includes countries ranked 1–48 and 143–189.

2. The top country on the list is Hong Kong. People born there in 2019 can expect to live 84.9 years. The last country on the list is the Central African Republic, where the 2019 birth cohort has a life expectancy of only 53.3 years. In other words, people in the countries at the top of the list can expect to live over thirty years longer than in the countries at the bottom.

   The countries where 2019 babies have the longest life expectancies are mostly in Europe and Asia. The countries with the shortest life expectancies are almost all in Africa.

   Women live longer than men in all of the countries on the list, on average about four to six years longer. In some countries near the bottom of the list, the difference drops to two or three years.

   Life expectancy seems to be closely related to wealth. The countries at the top of the list are generally rich ones, and the ones at the bottom are poor. One exception is the US. Although it's one of the world's richest countries, it's number 37 in life expectancy.

Step 3

It would be interesting to know more about the factors that influence life expectancy. Wealth is certainly the most important one. Others probably include the environment, the political situation (wars lead to earlier deaths), and the availability of affordable health care.

I didn't think there were any big surprises in the list except for the position of the US. It's below Barbados and only one place above Cuba. I think that the cost of health care in the United States probably plays a role here.

I would also like to see how these numbers have changed over the years. How much life expectancy have countries gained … or even lost? What countries have changed the most?

TABLE 3

Generation Alpha

The title of this table is 'Generation Alpha'. It compares eight characteristics of the last six generations. The source of the table is McCrindle.

This is a very large, colourful, fun table with lots of symbols. Each column has a different main colour and is about a different generation of the last 75 years. Each row presents information about that generation's name, slang terms, and favourite objects. This allows easy comparison of the different generations. Symbols visualise the age of each generation and the different kinds of cars, toys, music devices, and screens associated with them.

This table is very unusual because it includes very few statistics. Instead, it shows a lot of qualitative data about each generation.

The symbols give valuable information about the items mentioned. Even if we don't know what a Model T Ford is, the symbol shows us that it is a very old-fashioned looking car. The symbols also make it easy to see how the music devices of each generation have become more technologically advanced.

The slang terms included are fun but hard to understand, probably even for some native speakers!

The diagrams included with each leadership style make it easy to understand how each style works. We see the development from a style in which the boss is above the employees to styles where the boss has a position parallel to the employees.

Most of the entries seem to be matters of opinion, not fact. It's usually hard to say in what year a generation starts and ends. The choice of slang terms can only be a few typical words. There are also certainly several toys associated with each generation.

This table is fun to look at and explore and gives some interesting information about each generation. It would be fun to find more categories for each generation!

VENN DIAGRAM 1

Avoid the Three Cs

Step 1

1. a) The title of this Venn diagram is 'Avoid the Three Cs: Be Aware of Different Levels of Risk in Different Settings'.

   b) The source of the diagram is the World Health Organization, Western Pacific Region.

   c) The Venn diagram has three circles. They are yellow, red, and blue.

   d) It gives information about places where COVID-19 spreads easily.

   e) The circles correspond to a large legend with pictures above the diagram. The yellow circle represents crowded places. The blue circle represents close-contact settings. The red circle represents confined and enclosed spaces.

Step 2

2. (1) shows • (2) grows • (3) intersections • (4) single • (5) line • (6) points • (7) three • (8) meaningful

Step 3

I think that this diagram shows very well how each factor increases your risk of getting COVID-19. However, I think it would be even better if each factor were labelled on the Venn diagram. Looking from the diagram to the legend is an extra step that some people might not take. Maybe it would have been possible to make the diagram larger and include the information from the legend in it.

VENN DIAGRAM 2

British Isles

Step 1

1. The title of this Euler diagram is 'British Isles'. The source is Wikimedia Commons.
2. There is one main set and several subsets that show the states and other legal entities of the British Isles. The major geographical features are green, and legal distinctions are blue.

Step 2

3. a) The largest set is the British Isles.
   b) There are six subsets. The subsets are British Islands, United Kingdom, Great Britain, Ireland, Crown Dependencies, and Channel Islands.
   c) The diagram shows five islands: Great Britain, Ireland, Isle of Man, Guernsey, and Jersey.
   d) Northern Ireland belongs to the island of Ireland geographically.
   e) Northern Ireland belongs to the United Kingdom politically.
   f) Scotland, Wales, and England belong to Great Britain.
   g) The crown dependencies of the British Isles are the Isle of Man, Guernsey, and Jersey.

Step 3

I think that this diagram shows the relationships of the British Isles very well. Although it doesn't give great detail, it shows the basic geographic and political features of the different places. It's sometimes hard to understand the distinctions between the United Kingdom, Great Britain, and the other places connected to them. This diagram gives a good overview.

I would add more detail about the different political entities and use different colours to do that.

VENN DIAGRAM 3

Trump's unique feat

The title of this Venn diagram is 'Trump's unique feat'. There is no source given for this diagram.

The diagram is made of three sets in overlapping circles. A blue circle on the top shows presidents who were impeached. A yellow circle on the left contains those who lost the popular vote but became president. A red circle on the right includes presidents who only served one term (but not those who died in office, did not run for a second term, or who became president after the death or resignation of the previous president).

Only three presidents have been impeached, and only five lost the popular vote but still became president. There are 12 presidents in the red circle (Served one term). Three intersections of two circles show which presidents fell into two of these categories. Three presidents are in the intersection of red and yellow. There is one president in the intersection of blue and red. However, there is only one president who belongs to all three categories: Donald Trump.

This diagram shows three ways to identify presidents who seem unpopular. The diagram does this by using three categories. The category 'Lost popular vote but became president' is because of the Electoral College in the US. The Electoral College is controversial because it makes it possible for a president to lose the popular vote but still win the election.

We can see that the category 'Served one term' should be examined closely because this doesn't always mean that a president wasn't popular. Impeachment can mean that the president was targeted by political enemies in Congress. It does not show that he was unpopular with the American people in general. Some people say that was the case with Bill Clinton, and Trump's supporters would say this also applied to him. The diagram was obviously designed to show Donald Trump in a particularly critical light.

More information about the presidents (years in office, date of impeachment etc.) would be interesting. I would also like to see what kind of Venn diagrams of presidents could be created with other categories.

INFOGRAPHIC 1

Top 5 Languages Spoken in Australia

Step 1

1. a) Top 5 Languages Spoken in Australia
   b) Australian Bureau of Statistics, 2016 Census of Population and Housing
   c) smiley face, speech bubbles
   d) the top five languages spoken in Australia, the percentage of people who speak that language, and the word 'hello' in that language

Step 2

2. The five languages in the speech bubbles are English only, Mandarin, Arabic, Vietnamese, and Cantonese. The largest is English, which is the only language spoken by most of the population. The next largest is Mandarin, followed by Arabic and Vietnamese and Cantonese.

   The great majority (72.7%) of Australians only speak English. The other four languages only add up to a total of 6.3%. That means that about a fifth of Australians either speak another language, speak more than one language, or didn't state a language.

   When you add together the people who speak Mandarin (2.5%) and Cantonese (1.2%), you can see that 3.7% speak a Chinese language. This means that there are probably a lot of people in Australia whose families originally came from China.

Step 3

It would be interesting to have the missing information about languages spoken by the 21% of Australians not included in this infographic. There must be a lot of languages that are spoken by a very small number of Australians. It's interesting that there are no Aboriginal languages in the top five.

I like the way that 'Hello' in each language is shown in the writing of that language: it gives a little extra information about each language.

INFOGRAPHIC 2

St Patrick's Day by the Numbers

Step 1

1. The title of this Infographic Is 'St Patrick's Day by the Numbers: The Numbers Behind St Patrick's Day in the US. The source of the infographic is Statista.

2.

behind	contains information	is illustrated by	in the US
4	2	7	6
about the numbers	**St Patrick's Day**	**three large symbols**	**The infographic**
3	5	8	1

The infographic about the numbers behind St Patrick's Day in the US is illustrated by three large symbols.

Step 2

3.

The background	The first symbol 	The second symbol 	The third symbol 
green with shamrocks	yellow buildings lines = river blue left/green right	clock five hours highlighted in dark green	three bags peace symbol = 1960s

4. The infographic has a green background with shamrocks on it. There are three symbols: yellow buildings with blue and green lines representing a river; a clock showing five hours highlighted in dark green; and three bags with peace symbols on them.

Step 2

5.

The background	The first symbol 	The second symbol 	The third symbol 
colour and symbol of Ireland (St Patrick's Day = Irish holiday)	river being dyed (blue to green)	dye lasts five hours	1960s = period in which river was first dyed

6. a) 7 • b) 3 • c) 5

7. The main colour of the infographic is green, which is the colour of Ireland. The shamrocks are a famous symbol of the country. The first symbol shows a river that goes from blue to green and the information that 40 pounds of is dye used to colour it. The five hours highlighted on the clock illustrate that the dye lasts for five hours. The bags of dye with peace signs on them are meant to symbolise the 1960s, which is the period in which the river was first dyed. Besides the amount of dye, the length of time, and the year, there are no other statistics in the infographic.

Step 3

8. I think that green and shamrocks were a natural choice for the design of this infographic. The three fun facts about St Patrick's Day in the US shows what an important holiday it is there. Probably a lot of people in Chicago had family who came to the US from Ireland many years ago. I didn't know that Chicago dyes the river green, but it sounds like a fun way to celebrate the holiday, even if you're not Irish!

INFOGRAPHIC 3

Dirty Beaches: 24 Hours of Trash

The title of this infographic is 'Dirty Beaches: 24 Hours of Trash'. It shows what types of trash were cleaned up on beaches around the world on one day.

The source of the information is the Ocean Conservancy. The infographic was created by Statista.

The infographic lists ten types of trash, each with a label and a symbol. A number above each symbol says how many pieces of this type of trash were found during the cleanup event. Cigarette butts (2,412,151) were the type of trash that was most frequently cleaned up and have the largest symbol. Foam takeout containers (580,570) were the least common of these ten types of trash and have the smallest symbol. The infographic lists a total of over ten million pieces of trash that were cleaned up during the event.

I think that listing the types of trash cleaned up is a good way to make people think about what they throw away. While some people might think that one little cigarette butt isn't a problem, over 2.4 million of them are a really big problem. It also might make people think about how they can stop making trash, for example, by drinking from reusable bottles and using cloth bags instead of plastic.

It would also be interesting to know the weight and volume of the trash. While there were a lot of cigarette butts, for example, each one is very small. It could be that 580,570 foam take-away containers weigh more or use more space than 2,412,151 cigarette butts.

I would expect that a lot of trash doesn't fit into one of these categories or is so old that people don't know what it was. It would be interesting to know how much other trash was collected.

Language to help you describe, analyse, and evaluate visuals

Function	Sample sentences	Tense / Form
Giving the title of the visual	*The title of this bar chart / infographic / … is …*	simple present
Giving a brief description of the visual	*It shows …*	simple present
Naming the source	*The source of the information is …* *The data in the chart comes from … and is based on the survey …*	simple present
	The chart was created by …	simple past passive
Description of the visual and its elements (lines, bars, segments, etc.)	*The … shows / visualises / represents …* *The legend gives …* *The colour of each … corresponds to …* *There is a …* *There are …*	simple present
	The … is divided into … *The … is made of …*	simple present passive
Description and analysis of the data The tense you use depends on what the data shows. Some visuals show a situation that has probably not changed much (for example, map 2 and Venn diagram 3). You can use the simple present to talk about them. If the visual shows something from the past (for example, line chart 1), use the simple past.	*The data shows that …* *Is / are / have …* *Was / were / had …*	simple present simple present simple past
Evaluation	*I think that …*	simple present
	I would like to know … *I didn't know …* *I didn't expect …* *I was surprised …* *It would be interesting to know …*	modal verb infinitive

Talking about numbers, data, and statistics

<table>
<tr><td rowspan="2">Describing sizes</td><td colspan="2">... is the ...
... are arranged from ...</td><td colspan="2">largest ...
smallest ...
most / least popular ...
greatest ...
highest / lowest ...</td></tr>
<tr><td colspan="2">All ...
Nearly all ...
Most of ...
About ...
Around ...</td><td colspan="2"></td></tr>
<tr><td>Comparing</td><td colspan="2">... is ...</td><td colspan="2">closely followed by...
almost the same as ...
(much) larger than ...
(much) less than ...
(much) more than ...
over ...
(much) higher than ...
(much) lower than ...</td></tr>
<tr><td rowspan="3">Numbers</td><td>almost
about
more than
less than
exactly</td><td>a tenth
one quarter
half
two thirds
three quarters</td><td>ten percent
twenty-five percent
fifty percent
sixty-six percent
seventy-five percent</td><td>one in ten
one in four
one in two
two in three
three in four</td></tr>
<tr><td colspan="2" rowspan="2">Points and commas are used the other way around in German and English</td><td>English</td><td>German</td></tr>
<tr><td>28.3%
one million =
1,000,000</td><td>28,3%
one million =
1.000.000</td></tr>
<tr><td rowspan="3">Trends</td><td colspan="2">to stay the same</td><td>to go up
to increase
to rise</td><td>to go down
to decrease
to fall</td></tr>
<tr><td colspan="4">slowly • quickly • steadily • gradually • steeply • greatly • significantly • a little bit • suddenly</td></tr>
<tr><td colspan="4">between ... and ... • from ... to ... • before • until • first • then</td></tr>
</table>

1. Auflage 2024 23 22 21

Alle Drucke dieser Auflage sind unverändert und können im Unterricht nebeneinander verwendet werden. Die letzte Zahl bezeichnet das Jahr des Drucks.

www.schuenemann-verlag.de | www.sprachzeitungen.de

Autorin: Rebecca Kaplan
Redaktion: Franziska Lange, Carol Richards, Anne-Kathrein Schiffer

Cover-Illustration: Getty Images
Gestaltung und Satz: Jens Buchholtz, Britta Leuchtmann
Printed in EU 2021 | ISBN 978-3-7961-1073-3